Our Journey Through High Functioning Autism and Asperger Syndrome

of related interest

Asperger's Syndrome
A Guide for Parents and Professionals
Tony Attwood
ISBN 1 85302 577 1

Pretending to be Normal
Living with Asperger's Syndrome
Liane Holliday Willey
ISBN 1 85302 749 9

The Self-Help Guide for Special Kids and their Parents
Joan Matthews and James Williams
ISBN 1 85302 914 9

I am Special
Introducing Children and Young People
to their Autistic Spectrum Disorder
Peter Vermeulen
ISBN 1 85302 916 5

Learning to Live with High Functioning Autism
A Parent's Guide for Professionals
Mike Stanton
ISBN 1 85302 915 7

Asperger Syndrome, the Universe and Everything
Kenneth Hall
ISBN 1 85302 930 0

Blue Bottle Mystery
An Asperger Adventure
Kathy Hoopmann
ISBN 1 85302 978 5

Our Journey Through High Functioning Autism and Asperger Syndrome

A Roadmap

Edited by Linda Andron

*Forewords by Tony Attwood
and Liane Holliday Willey*

Jessica Kingsley Publishers
London and Philadelphia

First published in the United Kingdom in 2001 by
Jessica Kingsley Publishers Ltd,
116 Pentonville Road,
London N1 9JB, England
and
325 Chestnut Street,
Philadelphia, PA 19106, USA.

www.jkp.com

Library of Congress Cataloging in Publication Data
A CIP catalog record for this book is available from the Library of Congress

British Library Cataloguing in Publication Data
A CIP catalogue record for this book is available from the British Library

ISBN 1 85302 947 5

Printed and Bound in Great Britain by
Athenaeum Press, Gateshead, Tyne and Wear

CONTENTS

*This book is dedicated to all the parents and children who have allowed me
to join them on the journey, to my late husband Steve who was in every sense
my partner, to my mother Ruth and daughters Carin and Shira, who have
always supported my efforts, and especially to my daughter Elana who has
chosen to join with me and the families on the journey that yet lies ahead.*

Foreword

In the first chapter, Jeannette Darlington writes about her sons Glen and Evan and that: "Sometimes I think I've learned more from them than they have from me. Whatever the truth of that, it's been an interesting and educational journey." The authors of this book have chosen an appropriate title. When you start reading, you embark on a journey of discovery. Jeannette's chapter explores areas of autism and Asperger Syndrome that are relatively unknown territory. The research literature makes little reference to imagination, humor and empathy yet parents and experienced clinicians know that individuals with an autistic spectrum disorder can develop an idiosyncratic imagination and a remarkable sense of humor and acquire, in certain circumstances, empathy for others. The developmental perspective and personal comments of Jeannette's sons are especially illuminating.

We are only just beginning to learn how to help other children to understand the perspective and abilities of the child with Asperger Syndrome and the chapter by Max Lisser and Jennifer Westbay entitled "Making Friends with Aliens" provides a valuable resource in the form of a booklet that will become a template for both parents and teachers. The material, in part, is an adaptation of the seminal work in this area by Carol Gray, and enables the child to identify and have recognized his or her unique qualities.

There can be a two-way breakdown in understanding and communication between ourselves and the person with Asperger's Syndrome. One way of improving communication is to learn "How to Speak Asperger's" and Fran Goldfarb's chapter could be considered as a foreign language guide for the journey.

The advice and translations are essential reading for parents and professionals.

We now recognize that when a child is diagnosed as having Asperger Syndrome, there is the distinct possibility that a close relative may have the same pattern of abilities and a similar developmental history. Learning that his son had the diagnosis led Jim Devine to realize that he shares some of the characteristics of his son. His chapter provides the perspective of a father and examines the thoughts and perceptions of an adult with Asperger Syndrome.

Jim Nye describes the development of his son, Calvin, who also provides his own comments on situations. The chapter ends with: "Calvin still accuses me of making him *not autistic,* especially when he is frustrated with being normal. He has his own *second smile* and has thanked me for helping him become who he is today. The fight was worth it." This chapter will be an inspiration for parents.

Linda Andron is a clinical social worker and specialises in autistic spectrum disorders; her chapter incorporates the academic and theoretical perspectives with those of parents and individuals with high functioning autism and Asperger Syndrome. She describes some of her programs for children and families and her insight and strategies will be particularly valuable for social workers and therapists.

Our Journey Through High Functioning Autism and Asperger Syndrome: A Roadmap is an excellent travellers' guide because it is written by people who have been there. The stories are enthralling and the authors' experiences enable us to understand the culture and perspective of people with an autistic spectrum disorder. This book is recommended for anyone who has embarked on a journey to explore a part of our world that we have only recently discovered.

Tony Attwood
September 2000

Foreword

"Have you ever heard of something called 'Asperger Syndrome'?" the doctor asked my husband and I the day we were called in to discuss the results of our daughter's battery of developmental, educational and psychological tests. We had. Down went my husband's head. Round went his shoulders. His heart was sad. Tears cooled my flushed cheeks. Non-stop jabbering flew from my mouth. My heart was happy. How we each reacted to the news was a clear reflection of how we viewed life at the time. When my husband heard the doctors describe the world of Asperger Syndrome, he heard troubling words that kept him racing for an idea which would make everything bad go away, everything difficult become easy, and everything different conform to the norm. He had much to learn. I, on the other hand, heard words that brought not only my daughter's actions and behaviors into clear focus, but also my own. At long last, I heard the words that would finally set me free and in so doing, would enable me to help my daughter find her own wings. No longer would I look in the mirror or in the eyes of my young daughter and suspect I was eye-to-eye with a schizophrenic, a neurotic, or a depressive. Our lives, I knew, were on the verge of something quite positive and exciting. We had Asperger Syndrome. I was not on the brink of mental disaster; I was on the brink of discovery. If only I had had this book with me then. How much faster I would have seen just how great the discovery.

To my mind, the advice I glean from doctors, therapists and teachers is precious and beneficial. I regularly turn to those with several diplomas on their walls, and years of experience under their feet, for their thoughts and suggestions. These people are, after all, the relatively objective voices who so often devote their professional lives, and then some, to helping those with special needs come to understand not only their limitations and their frustrations, but also their potential and their capabilities. These experts are, naturally, the first line most of us with children on the autism spectrum turn to when we turn to anyone for answers. But, when those of us with special needs people in our lives are lucky enough to find them, we turn to those who are the real experts, the real voices of reason and understanding, the only people in the world who can truly share in our dreams and our realities. We turn to those whose life experiences mirror our own; the parents and the people with special needs themselves. These are the voices we know we can trust and depend on. They are the voices who speak out in this book. They are voices well worth listening to.

I had a great many of my hunches and hopes confirmed when I read the words of the generous parents, and their even more generous children, who contributed to this book. I learned that there are those affected by Asperger Syndrome who view their wondrous world as good and decent, as fun and funny, as interesting and valuable, and as commendable and admirable. I also learned a good many new strategies I can copy and apply to help my own Asperger daughter as she strives to make new friendships, speak neurotypical speech, understand empathy and humor, use her rich imagination fruitfully, and come to terms with who she really is. Most important, I learned it is possible to be inspired to see the glass as half full, no matter how many leaks there seem to be in the cup. I thank the authors of this book for reminding me we are what we make of ourselves.

I believe the community who reads this book will join me in thanking those who wrote it, for their courage, their wit and their plethora of fine ideas.

Liane Holliday Willey, EdD
September 2000

Our Different Journey –
An Introduction

In the pages that follow, you will meet parents and children and join them on their journey. For all it has been a journey different from what they expected. Different and yet not without its joys and rewards. For some it has been a journey from silence to speech. For many it has been a journey from denial to sharing their difference with others. It has been a journey from isolation to lasting friendship. It has been a journey of self-discovery for both parents and children. It has been a journey that has required learning to understand a different way of seeing the world, a different way of communicating, in sum a different culture. For all the journey continues. The final destination of these children and families still lies ahead.

It has been my great pleasure to accompany these families on their journey. I have learned a great deal from them and grown both professionally and personally. The families you will meet in this book are excellent representatives of the over five hundred families that have participated in our family support program. The program began 10 years ago with five families in a small room at UCLA. I asked myself what was our purpose, what were we hoping to accomplish. At that time, I believed we could catalog a group of skills and teach them systematically. It was my hope that this would lead the children to the 'normalcy' everyone sought and allow them to become totally included with other children. But our funding sources said that this did not fall under their jurisdiction and asked that we provide family support. And so, I began the journey of coming to know these families and the support that they would need and give to each other. Over the last

10 years, our program has grown to serve as many as three hundred families at a time at nine far flung sites. And my knowledge of their strength and courage has grown exponentially. At each site, a group of families gathers once a week for only one hour. But the connections that occur are far reaching. The knowledge that is shared is immense. I have learned that all members of the family need support – parents, siblings, and children alike – and that being able to teach a list of "social skills" is a myth. I have learned that the need for support is ongoing. All of us must walk together on this journey. We must walk side by side. There is strength in numbers.

The experience of all these families has left me feeling very hopeful about the journey. By and large, the children are doing well. They have grown intellectually and socially. They are on their way to independent living and having interesting jobs. Their sensory sensitivities have decreased and their adaptive skills increased. They are learning to manage their anxieties. They have learned to tolerate change and, yes, they even attend school dances with loud music. They have learned when to laugh, try desperately to understand conventional humor, and are uniquely funny in their own way. They have a wonderful and rich imagination, albeit often quite odd. They care deeply about their friends and are very empathetic, when they can understand what the other is experiencing. They have a great sense of social justice. They are indeed different. It is fundamental to who they are and most have no desire to change this. They want others to accept them, but do not want to be "fixed." They are coming to understand that they must behave in certain conventional ways to be accepted in society, but they want others to understand and respect their unique way of seeing the world. Their families and the professionals who have had the pleasure of working with them have grown as the result of living with these children.

It is all of this that led us to talk about putting together this book. It is our desire to share some of the unique qualities of these children, to dispel some of the myths and to celebrate difference.

At the same time, it is important to us to share the obstacles families have had to climb over on their journey. We have attempted to draw a roadmap for others to follow. While we could only include the experiences of five families in our program, we believe that these represent the experiences of many. We hope that as you turn these pages you will resonate with our experience. We hope you may also find hope, as I have, in the signposts these families have passed. For each of you the journey will be somewhat different, as it has been for each of our families. For some, like Glen and Evan, it has been a journey that began with classic autism. Each step along the way was greeted by applause from all concerned. For Josh, on the other hand, it was a long while before the correct diagnosis was found. Children like Josh, instead of being told how great they are, have been told how rude and oppositional they are. For Max, there was an early recognition of problems as well as growth. The time he spent trying to be a square peg in a round hole was difficult. But once the hole was made big enough, he could fit in well. Guthrie's diagnosis led to his father's recognition of his own Asperger's characteristics. For Calvin and his father, it was a journey that has led to a "second smile." When he was eight, he asked Jim if he could sleep with him one night. Jim asked "Why?" Calvin replied that it was because he loved him. Jim asked why Calvin always said he hates him. Calvin protested that he did not hate his dad, but really loved him. He went on to say that Jim had been really mean to him and yelled at him. Jim asked him when that happened. Calvin replied "When I was little and acted "crazy." When asked if he knew why he had acted "crazy," Calvin answered, "I just had to be." At that early point in the journey, Calvin did not have the language to tell Dad what was happening and how he was feeling. But later, as his language developed, he could look back on it with a smile. From Calvin we learn, that the children are aware of much that is happening on the journey, even if they cannot narrate it for us until much later.

For all of us the road has not been clearly laid out. There have been many crossroads. Each family has needed to decide which interventions to pursue and how much time and money to devote to each. They have had to weigh and measure the value of different educational placements. In all of these decisions, they have been faced with many conflicting theories and the promises of "cure." They have struggled with decisions about who and what to tell about their children's differences. They have been faced with trying to help their children grow and change without giving up who they fundamentally are. This has also led them to ask who they are and what is most important to them.

We do not presume to tell you which road to take. We cannot promise what you will find at the end of each road. We can only hope that the roadmap we have drawn as we go will give you some signposts to follow as you move ahead.

Most people think that children with autism and Asperger's cannot express humor and imagination and do not have empathy. Jeannette and her family will share the roadmap they have developed for this. You will learn how to assist children in understanding and developing humor, expressing their imagination and tuning in to the feelings of others.

If we cannot teach "social skills" *per se*, how do we help children develop the tools they need to interpret the places they will visit and live in on their journeys? I have tried to provide you with a roadmap that shows the pitfalls of this journey and, at the same time, provides signposts that can help these children.

Friendship is one of the most fundamental things we all seek. While children with autism and AS often want to be alone, they do crave relationships with others. It is important that these relationships are with others who share their interests and that they are fostered by adults who can nurture their development. The roadmap for the development of such a friendship is poignantly related by Ruth.

The relationship between parent and child is at the heart of the journey we all take through life. When a child cannot communicate, it is hard to know what path to follow. While it may seem that the child is in his own world and does not see life as it passes by, we may find that, in reality, he has been quietly observing. It is this reality that Jim shares with us.

Children with autism and AS are like foreign students. They are in need of interpreters and tour guides for their journey. Learning how to speak Asperger's is a prerequisite for accompanying these children. Fran will offer you her lexicon for this part of the journey. On the journey to understand the children, parents begin to look at their own ways of dealing with the world. Often they find many of the same differences in themselves. Jim helps us to understand how this happened to him. He gives us a first hand account of his own journey and how it has informed his understanding of his son.

When and how we share our differences with others is a critical concern on the journey. Jennifer and Max will share the guidebook they developed and give you a map for developing your own.

So, we ask you to join us on our journey. We ask you to let us draw for you a map that may well lead you on a different journey than you might have expected or planned, but one that has its unique rewards. We hope that your journey will take you and those you love to places you do not believe possible.

1

Humor, Imagination
and Empathy in Autism

Jeannette Darlington
with Evan and Glen Darlington

Autism, Evan and Glen

> He that has patience may compass anything
>
> – François Rabelais *Gargantua and Pantagnel*

Every once in a while, I notice Glen galloping around the house, drumming at the air with his hands and squealing softly, and think, *that's really kind of strange.* But most of the time, I don't even think about it. It's Glen. It's something he does.

Sometimes I see Evan, standing at the edge of a group, just watching, and wish he could step in and contribute his own ideas. But mostly, I'm just glad he's with a group and listening. He's not at the center, but he is taking part.

In all, both of my sons have come a long way, and so have I. Sometimes I think I've learned more from them than they have from me. Whatever the truth of that, it's been an interesting and educational journey.

Autism

Autism varies a lot from one person to another. Even in my own two sons the symptoms differ, but there is always the same triad of impairments, that is, impairments in the same three areas:

- language/communication
- social functioning
- restricted interests and/or repetitive patterns of behavior.

Specific diagnostic criteria also vary, but the experts agree that these are the main areas to look at.

Cognitive development (intelligence) is commonly in the retarded range, but individuals with autism can have average or even gifted IQ's. Several genetic disorders, such as tuberous sclerosis, fragile X and phenylketonuria, are associated with autism, and often, but not always, those affected are also retarded.

While the lack of imagination is not an official symptom of autism, many early researchers believed imagination was missing from individuals with autism. More recent research indicates that not only imagination but a sense of humor and even empathy can be present, although they are often not well developed.

Language/Communication

In my own children, the language impairments were obvious. At three, Evan did not respond to language at all, although he did have a very limited single-word vocabulary – all nouns – that only I could understand. Glen had a wider spoken vocabulary at three than his brother had at that age, but he didn't seem to understand what I said to him any better. Neither one of them could answer a simple yes-or-no question with a simple yes or no until age seven, although Glen did start talking to people a little when he was six.

I remember visiting Glen's school when he was in the first grade. He was in a special day class for high functioning autistic kids. While I was there, his teacher asked him, "What comes out of a volcano?" Glen proceeded to give a dissertation on every-thing he knew about a volcano, couched in disjointed phrases he had probably read in a book or heard from his teacher.

Glen was what is known as *echolalic*. He could repeat words and phrases he had heard from others in fair imitation of the original speaker. From when he was about five until he was nine or so, he had what I call "cut-and-paste echolalia." He would put together phrases he'd learned to form complete thoughts, but the pattern of his speech was very peculiar because of this method of construction. Not only did he use phrases that sounded very advanced, the rhythm and tone of his speech were oddly mismatched – my sister commented he sounded just like an automated voice telephone message. The way automated systems patch together bits of recordings to give an approximation of live speech is very similar to the way Glen put together his phrases.

One feature of autistic language that occurs in a significant number of cases is pronoun reversal. The classic form of this is referring to oneself as "you" and others as "I." Evan never did this, possibly because he didn't use pronouns much until he had that particular neural connection pretty well developed. But Glen did. His "I–you" reversal was sporadic, because he too didn't use pronouns much during the time he was prone to the error, but at six he reversed "he" and "she" almost to perfection. He also put his underwear on backward pretty consistently. I don't think there was a fundamental confusion in his mind about who he was (the reason often given for pronoun reversal), nor was there a random difficulty – I think the wiring in that specific part of his brain was reversed somehow.

At the time of writing, Glen is fourteen and has a very mature and somewhat pedantic style of speech. Last night I overheard him say that when he got a car he would probably get a used one, "because of my parents' economic nature."

Evan, at seventeen, has long had a vocabulary beyond his years, but you have to know him very well and pay careful attention or you'll never hear it. He doesn't talk much, and he's generally so overstressed when he's in public that he won't talk at all. I took him to the Department of Motor Vehicles yesterday to get him an identification card (so he can actually use the credit card he got last week), and I'm sure they thought he was retarded. At least they treated him very gently. He responded to me a little while we were waiting in line, but he didn't say anything, not even a grunted monosyllable, to anybody else. When Evan talks, it's late at night, when I'm about to drop into bed. Apparently he has done this at camp too, and utterly astonished everybody. They heard more communication from him between eleven and midnight one night than they had heard from him in the last seven years.

Social Functioning

I remember one occasion when I took Glen and Evan to a mothers' meeting at someone else's house. Glen was not quite one-and-a-half years old, while Evan was almost four. When we got there, Evan went to the edge of the room and lay down on the carpet facing the wall, while Glen proceeded to treat all the mothers as if they were his own personal climbing structures. Neither of my sons paid any attention to the other children at all.

My two children represented the extremes of three social styles exhibited by autistic children: aloof (Evan), passive, and active-but-odd (Glen).

Today Evan spends much of his time in a passive state (he hovers at the edges of groups and observes). He withdraws only occasionally when the world's stimuli become too much for him to handle. Some people imagine such children withdrawing to rich dream worlds, but apparently this wasn't the case for Evan when he was younger. He was thirteen when he observed, "When I was little, life was like a badly-edited movie. It jumped." It seems that, when he went away, he didn't go anywhere – he went dormant.

Glen is still mostly active-but-odd – except when he's reading, and then he is totally absorbed. He still tends to barge through situations without paying much attention to other people, even if he has improved in this regard. On the other hand, he can stand in front of an auditorium full of adults and give a speech without any appearance of self-consciousness.

In his own quiet way Evan is just as weird as Glen, but Glen is so much more demonstrative that he can make other kids uncomfortable. Among other things, when he is even mildly excited, Glen may jump up and down, flap his hands and make funny noises. He can also be supremely oblivious to other people. While Evan is always observing, if seldom joining in, Glen tends to move through the world with a sublime disregard for others. It's as if Evan sees life as a spectator sport, while Glen treats it more like a game of solitaire.

A certain amount of the social difficulty encountered by people with autism is due to "theory of mind" deficits. Essentially, a theory of mind is what enables an individual to realize that other people do not necessarily know what he knows or think what he thinks. Some researchers believe such deficits are a fundamental root of autistic disorders. Even if there's more to autism, this theory explains a lot.

One of the tests for theory of mind is called the "Sally-Anne Test." The tester uses two dolls (one called Sally, the other named Anne), a marble, a box and a covered basket. The test starts with both dolls and all the objects in the same "room." Sally has a prized marble, which she puts in the box, and then she leaves the room. Anne now takes the marble and puts it into the basket, but outwardly everything looks as it did when Sally left. Now the tester brings Sally back and asks the child, "Where will Sally look for her marble?"

Most four-year-olds have no problem with this test. At eleven, Evan insisted Sally would look in the basket – where he knew it was, rather than where Sally had put it. Even when I pressed him, asking, "Where would Sally expect to find her marble?" he was adamant. Of course, this was the child who, at almost nine, raised my hand to his forehead and asked *me* where he hurt.

Glen was nine when he did the Sally-Anne test, and his first response was very autistic. This explained something that had puzzled me a couple of years before. Glen had a story book about Donald Duck's Uncle Scrooge in which Scrooge followed a trail of pennies, expecting to find a treasure, but at the end of the trail he found a surprise party in his honor. Once Glen knew the ending – and in spite of the fact that Scrooge stated on almost every page, "There must be a treasure," – he insisted on all later readings that Scrooge thought he was going to find a party. However, by the time he was nine, Glen was able to think about the Sally-Anne situation a while and decide, without prompting, that Sally would look in the box after all.

Then there's the matter of social communication. People with autism tend to take things very literally. One day about a year ago, Glen came home and claimed he had been humiliated at school and did not want to go the next day. I looked into the situation and discovered he had been going through the rehearsal for something called a "pin and ribbon" ceremony. One of the teachers had told everybody to "Pick up your feet and step lively." So Glen did, and one of his favorite teachers called him down for acting like Bozo the Clown. Glen was crushed. He hadn't been doing it to be funny, he had simply been following directions. Then, to make things worse, Glen went back to his seat and burst into tears. The biggest boy in the eighth grade class isn't supposed to cry, and some other teacher made a remark about that.

I called Glen's autism teacher and determined that the pin and ribbon ceremony was intended to remind students that their grades and behavior needed to be good enough, or they wouldn't qualify for eighth grade graduation. So I kept Glen home, and not only from the pin and ribbon ceremony, but from the "graduation" ceremony in June as well. All the school people thought Glen ought to participate in the graduation, but Glen didn't want to risk that kind of humiliation again, and I agreed with him.

Behavioral/Repetitive Rituals

A lot of things get tossed into the third diagnostic domain, and for some people with autism, this is their most significant area of difficulty. For instance, falling down, kicking and screaming, head-banging and self-injurious tantrums can be a problem for some children. Glen, who was a master of such displays, has pretty well grown past that stage, which is fortunate, since I can't pick him up and dump him in the middle of the living room any more. He hasn't bitten himself since he was ten, and he hasn't scratched his own face since he was eight or so (and the scars from that are pretty much hidden in the acne now).

Only once – when he was six – did Evan exhibit a falling-down, kicking and screaming tantrum, which absolutely astonished his teacher. Care to guess what set him off? One of the kids was in the wrong place in line.

There's a lot more to this category than tantrums, though. The way Evan got so upset about someone not being in his assigned place is just one example. Glen's inability to skip a question he can't answer is another, related symptom. In second grade, Glen had to fill out a simple questionnaire in his new class. The third or fourth question was "What is your phone number?" He couldn't answer it and refused to go to the next question, which was something he did know. Someone had to go find out his phone number, because only when that blank had been filled in was Glen able to continue. Even in high school, Glen doesn't like going past questions he can't answer, and we've had some unpleasant scenes involving impossible homework problems. He did mention recently that skipping a question might be a good thing to do sometimes, but I don't know if he has actually ever done it.

This inability to do things out of order can also pose problems in a social context. Glen went to a dance when he was almost eleven, and he had decided he was going to dance with a particular girl. When a beautiful blonde from the gifted program asked him to dance with her, he wouldn't do it – maybe even *couldn't* do it – until he had danced with his "dream girl" – who refused to dance with him. He cried all the way home because he didn't get to dance. He had his expected order all planned out, and when it wasn't possible for him to follow the intended sequence, he was unable to get past the problem.

Autistic people have very intense interests, often in somewhat bizarre things. The keynote speaker at a conference I once attended had a son who collected Reese's Peanut Butter Cup wrappers from different places. Except for the location where they were purchased, carefully recorded on the wrapper, the wrappers were all identical.

My own children don't have quite such unusual fixations, but both have certainly demonstrated intense interests. When Evan was younger, he was very interested in maps, which is not uncommon among people with autism. At nine, he could not only name the capital of every state, he could identify every state in the United States by its *shape*. He had atlases, map books, maps, geography games, you name it. Then we started working on getting him interested in the things that *came* from the places on the maps. After that, he discovered people and cultures from other countries. At the time of writing, Evan is very interested in cultural anthropology and material culture. He has quite a nice collection of Native American (Indian) art and artifacts, and he has even learned a few words of Cherokee as well as some dances.

Evan also collects coins, but not by date and mint. He collects for variety, and he has boxes and drawers of different coins, alphabetized by their country of origin.

His collection of 1:18 scale diecast metal cars is quite impressive too, although he doesn't spend hours dusting them any more. Now he's more likely to leave them in their boxes. He has found they stack much better that way.

Glen is not so much a collector of *things*. His passions express themselves more in the information he accumulates. He has every *Cartoon Guide to Whatever* in print, including *Statistics*, and he likes to quote from them. He has some insights to history not normally taught before college level classes and he could rattle off Newton's laws of physics when he was nine.

One time, when he was ten, the family went to the Reagan Presidential Library to see a special exhibit. Glen had already seen it, so he insisted on waiting in the lobby. I figured he probably wouldn't get into any trouble, so I let him, but I was rather apprehensive when one of the docents approached me and asked if that was my son out in the lobby. Wondering to myself what mischief he had gotten into, I admitted that he was. The man smiled. "He's a walking encyclopedia!" he exclaimed. "He's been telling me all kinds of things."

Glen also has almost every kind of construction toy known to humankind – Lego, Knex, Construx, Kapla Blocks, Robotix and a few others I can't remember at the moment. He is always glad to get another Lego kit, and he has been known to buy a $15 kit because it has *one* special part he needs for a project. If Legoland California were closer (it's a two to three hour drive), I'd get him an annual pass and drop him off there for a few hours every weekend.

Fortunately, my kids have both developed interests which, while a little unusual in their intensity, are not especially unusual in kind. On top of that, it makes it really easy for family and friends to figure out what to get them for their birthdays.

Stereotypical behavior, also called stimming (from stimulation) is also part of this domain. Evan is hypoactive (the opposite of hyperactive), so his stims are less obvious than Glen's, but he has a few. He curls his hands and rolls his wrists and sometimes (not as often as he once did) he makes "fish lips." Lately, as his coordination has improved, he has taken up playing with a yo-yo. This has the advantage that it is currently a popular pastime with others his age.

Glen is hyperactive. When he gets excited, for example when watching someone else play a game at an arcade, he jumps up and down, flaps his hands and squeals softly. As you may imagine, this garners him a few stares. But even when he is just waiting for an Internet web page to download, he often gets up from his chair and runs from one end of the house to the other. He weighs some

240 pounds (and is over six feet tall), so it sounds like an elephant jumping around. I keep expecting plaster to fall from the ceiling downstairs. In fact, on one occasion the globe on the lamp over the breakfast table was jarred loose by his galumphing above, and it crashed and broke spectacularly.

Cognitive

When Evan was little, he had a coloring card with outlines of balloons on it. Each balloon was labeled with a different color, and the child was supposed to color the balloons with crayons. Evan typically slashed one, skinny stripe of crayon across each balloon, but it was always the appropriate color. I used this when Evan was not quite four to demonstrate why I thought he wasn't retarded to a psychologist who had given him that diagnosis. "He's three years old and starting to *read*," I insisted. "That's not consistent with *my* view of mental retardation." I guess that it wasn't consistent with her view of retardation either, because she gave Evan a non-verbal test that showed him to be slightly on the positive side of average intellectually.

Then, when Glen was not quite two years old, I saw him scribbling happily away at Evan's balloon color card. I was glad that he wasn't drawing on the walls for a change, but just imagine my surprise when I saw that every scribble was the proper color for the balloon it was on! Glen can almost take his pick of IQ's – from borderline retarded to highly gifted – depending on the test and the time it was given.

At one time, Evan had a diagnosis of neurofibromatosis type 1 (NF1). This was because he had a growth on his brainstem along with the café au lait patches that frequently occur in NF. He eventually needed two surgeries for the brain tumor, which turned out to be a pilocytic astrocytoma. No further symptoms of NF1 have ever appeared, so it is probable he doesn't actually have that genetic disorder.

Imagination, Humor and Empathy

Most children learn language and social interaction intuitively, simply by observing and following examples. Evan and Glen needed to be systematically taught these things. By the same token, it has also been necessary to guide their discovery of imagination, humor and empathy.

The rest of this chapter goes into more detail about how Evan and Glen developed imagination, a sense of humor and the beginnings of empathy. The cartoon illustrations were stories I drew as a parental assignment for Evan's preschool/kindergarten severe speech and language disorders special day class. Every weekday, each student's parents were supposed to do a story, complete with pictures, concerning what happened at home that evening. The child took the story to school the next day to share

Figure 1.1: What happened at home? This is an early Evan and Glen cartoon. Since the stories were written for Evan and from his point of view, I often used Glen to demonstrate the wrong way to do things. Glen frequently obliged me in this regard.

with his classmates; the teacher used these picture stories as the basis for a language lesson. I did not do Evan and Glen cartoons every day, since they were rather demanding, but I averaged about two a week over the course of more than three years.

The *What happened at home?* cartoons taught far more than language, although they were excellent for that too. I used them in the same way the teacher used the corresponding *What happened at school?* stories to reinforce whatever lesson the class was working on. But I also included other things that seemed important, like imagination, humor and empathy.

Imagination and Play

> The great instrument of moral good is the imagination.
> – Percy Bysshe Shelley, *A Defense of Poetry* (1821)

Toys

When Glen was born, one of my friends decided the older brother should get a present, too, and gave Evan a red plastic car. He loved that car. He carried it around the way I would have

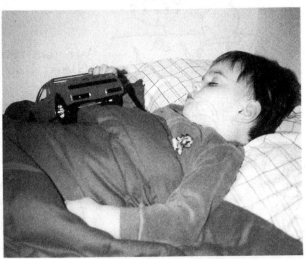

Figure 1.2: The Teddy Car. Evan really liked cars. For several years, he was seldom without a toy of some kind in his hand. This bright red one was the one he liked best from the time he got it at two-and-a-half until he discovered metal trucks at four years old.

expected him to carry a stuffed animal (but never did), and he even took it to bed with him the first night. We called it the teddy car.

Evan didn't make engine noises and roll it on the ground when he played with it – he was more likely to turn it over and spin the wheels. When he graduated to the little Hot Wheels and Matchbox metal cars, he continued turning them over and spinning their wheels, but he also added a new dimension of play. He sometimes lined the cars up along the seat of the sofa next to the arm, while at other times he would arrange them in parking-lot configurations.

Play is an excellent way to develop imagination, but autistic children often do not instinctively understand imaginative play and may need some modeling. For instance, on his fourth birthday, Evan got a Hot Wheels City play set. Although he played with it a lot, he usually put cars at the top of the ramp and simply let them roll down. He probably just liked watching the cars roll. I seriously doubt if he imagined himself driving – but in a cartoon recording his play, I attributed that motive to him. Basically I used the drawing to tell Evan that he could pretend he was driving the car.

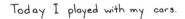

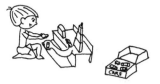

Figure 1.3: Hot Wheels City. Imagining driving a car was probably easier for Evan since he had driven the little cars at Disneyland. The picture of him driving the car here is, in fact, a direct tracing from a story about him driving a car at Disneyland.

Evan was also interested in rockets as well as cars. He watched a video of Disney's *Man in Space* over and over and he loved the toy rocket his dad brought back from a business trip. I combined the two in a story about Evan's imaginary journey to space, which I reported in the *What happened at home?* journal as if it had really happened. Evan – and his classmates – loved the story. My original intention in writing the story was to teach Evan about the planets, but by taking him on such an exciting journey in imagination, I demonstrated for him how much fun pretending can be. He not only looked through the storybook about his imaginary adventure many times, but it was one of the few books he wanted me to read to him.

When faced with an autistic child with a strong fixation, some people will try to redirect the child's interests, even to the extent of removing all objects of the fixation from his environment.

Figure 1.4: My Space Adventure. Evan had driven a car, but he had never been to space. In this case, I very loosely based the story on a video the kids liked to watch, but I put Evan in the place of the hero. This was definitely a stretch of the imagination. Glen loved this story, too, even though he wasn't in it.

Temple Grandin, a very able adult with autism, indicates from her own experience that this is more likely to induce anxiety than change the child's interests. Instead, such intense interests can, and should, be used as a hook to draw the child into more general pursuits.

Early on, I used Evan's interest in cars and rockets because it was a way to capture his attention. Later, when both kids discovered wooden trains, I made sure they had wooden people, too. Glen treated them largely as so much ballast, or even projectiles, but Evan was careful to load up the merry-go-round and the circus train with passengers. This may well have been because that was how they were depicted on the boxes, but it still got Evan to incorporate human figures in his play.

I have met few people with autism who are not interested in Lego construction sets. Even children who have little under-standing of language may be able follow the pictorial directions included with each set. Even more, there is something about construction toys in general, and Lego bricks in particular, that appeals to children with pervasive developmental disorders. Personally, I like the feel both of the bricks themselves and of the satisfying "snap" when I lock them together. Beyond that purely tactile enjoyment, the versatile and interchangeable design of the various elements satisfies what I might consider a sense of engineering aesthetics. Perhaps on some level, these are the same things that make Lego so popular with autistic children.

Left to his own devices, Evan would build the model according to the instructions, and if it had wheels, turn it over and spin them. Glen also built kits, but when they came apart (as, with Glen, they inevitably did) he put them together in different ways, though always as vehicles. He stuck the little mini-figures in where he needed pilots, but he never actually played with the people... until I got the Lego Pirate Ship.

I have a distinct advantage over many parents because I like toys myself. I can't say I'm tremendously interested in playing with them, but I'm the one who wanted the Pirate Ship. After some internal rationalizing, I got it, built it and encouraged the kids to play with it. At first, we had just the one ship, with numerous pirates. The interactions between these toy people may not have been the stuff of polite society, but they were appropriate to the context and demonstrated valuable play skills. While Evan and Glen's language and complexity of play were well below age level, Lego battles are something that can be (and are) enjoyed even by reasonably normal (if not necessarily typical) teens. I once spoke with a bright young man who wished he had brought some of his Lego sets with him to college.

Figure 1.5: Glenzilla. Glen is depicted as a disruptive influence in more than one cartoon. I was not making this up. He started walking at ten months of age and was running (on his toes) by his first birthday. He had two speeds: full and off.

Dramatic Play

From a fairly early age, Glen began fulfilling the proper role of younger brother – wanting to play with big brother but not knowing how. Although Evan could hardly interact with any other child, and in spite of the fact that Glen could be difficult (up to and including biting Evan), Evan had been fascinated by his baby brother from the beginning. For his part, Glen may have seen Evan as an intriguing toy.

For whatever reasons, they felt comfortable together. As a result, they sometimes played together, although not quite as nicely as I depicted them in our cartoons. If they interacted once, for thirty seconds, I would probably choose that to record in the day's *What happened at home?* I wanted them to remember those things and repeat them, or at least think that they were good.

Gas Station

Glen   is   in   the   car.

I put gas in the car.

Next it is my turn to drive.

9-23-87

Figure 1.6: Evan's Gas Station. We had a lot of toys. Some of them – like this car – the kids played with a lot. Some of them – like the gas pump – were used only occasionally. Others (notably stuffed animals) held almost no interest for Evan and Glen.

Evan's Gas Station was a good example of what could happen when Glen and Evan happened to be interested in the same set of toys. Evan was filling the tank of his car, and Glen jumped in. At that time, Evan had no possessiveness about anything – his teacher called me a year later to gleefully report the first occasion where he refused to share a toy – so whatever he may have felt about it, he let little brother get away with the carjacking. When I made my cartoon, though, I wrote it up as if they had planned the entire scenario.

Magicians do magic.
I put a rabbit in the hat.
I got my wand from Glen.
He was my assistant.

I did magic.
I made a flower appear.

4-29-87

Figure: 1.7: The Magic Show. This is rather wordy. Many of the early stories had more words than some of the later ones because Evan couldn't understand the words anyway. When Evan was four, the words were mostly for the benefit of the other students in his class.

Their more usual style of play is illustrated in the magician cartoon. Evan had a toy magic wand. When he pressed the two halves together, a small red flower appeared at one end. He could sit for hours shortening and extending the wand, watching the flower appear and disappear.

On the particular occasion recorded in the cartoon, he was inspired by *Mickey's Magic Show,* a Disney animated short he had seen on television.

I had made Evan a magician suit the previous year for Halloween; he took me by the wrist to where it was hanging in the closet. Because he still couldn't dress himself, I put the costume on him. Then, with my help, he assembled the other items he needed. While Evan was occupied setting up his show, Glen got the prized magic wand. I depict the two of them pulling on it, but Evan was not actually this assertive. He tried to get the wand from Glen, but when Glen held tight, Evan gave up, although he wasn't happy about it. I intervened, and the show went on.

Glen and I played cards.

Glen said, "Hi, fellas!"

5-7-90

Figure 1.8: "Hi, fellas!" By the time I did this cartoon, I was getting rather tired of cartooning. I sketched in a single panel, made a few notes in the margin about Glen's inspiration, and called it good enough. Evan was seven years old at this time, and Glen was almost five – old enough to at last have a full head of hair as well as an interest in costumes.

Both of my kids have always liked to wear the proper uniform for any given job, as Evan demonstrated when he wanted his magician suit in order to put on a magic show. Glen didn't particularly care about costumes then – after all, he wasn't even two years old yet – but at three, he started to become aware of them. As he approached age five, he had become very interested. Again, inspired by an animated short (starring Goofy this time rather than Mickey Mouse), Glen put on a jacket in order to play cards with Evan. He even spoke a line from the cartoon: "Hi, fellas!" This was what Goofy said when he took his place at the poker table with the guys.

Figure 1.9: Thanksgiving Rendezvous. At what age does a child become too old for dress-up? Never.

I made sure the kids had numerous costumes to wear at any given time. These ranged from cheap straw cowboy hats and bandanas to authentic *Star Trek: The Next Generation* uniforms from a costume shop. Glen had a white lab coat (long since outgrown) for when he did science experiments, and Evan had complete Northern Plains regalia to wear to Indian powwows and living history rendezvous. For anyone who wonders at what age a child becomes too old to wear costumes, consider the handsome gentleman in the picture with Evan. This is my father, who has yet to grow too old to wear them.

Costumed or not, Evan and Glen's early dramatic play relied heavily on outside influences. At one point, they were both very fond of a funny educational video about letters, and their favorite segment featured a "letter machine." The machine worked fine at first, but as it was made to go faster and faster, it started to malfunction. It finally exploded in a shower of cardboard cutout letters that pelted the hapless puppet actors. One day, the kids started to trade lines memorized from this scene. Their speech was not clear, but their cadences matched the exchange on the tape; when they faltered, I would prompt with a line of dialog until they arrived at the grand, slapstick finale. This was the first thing remotely resembling a conversation Glen and Evan had ever had. I think Glen was six by then, while Evan was about eight. For a long time, their somewhat infrequent dramatic play tended to be very derivative, with little evidence of creativity. Then, following his second brain surgery, Evan asked for and got a video camera from the Make-A-Wish Foundation. One of his first videos was *The Psychiatrist*, in which Glen portrays a psychiatrist complete with phony German accent, and Evan plays a succession of increasingly strange patients. I was the camera operator, and although I managed to keep from laughing out loud, there are places where the camera is a little wobbly because I was literally shaking with suppressed laughter.

Although they would not simply "play," they would perform for the camera. I still don't know what all of the influences for this delightful little comedy were, but I recognized enough of them to know that they weren't simply copying or mimicking. They were adapting and creating.

Creativity

The essence of creativity involves seeing an old thing in a new way, a process that rigid thought patterns can make very difficult. One of the earliest signs of creative thought in Evan and Glen is beautifully illustrated by their novel way of playing with a wooden train set (which would, no doubt, appall the European manufacturer). The ability to use something in a way suggested by its form rather than dictated by its actual nature or intended purpose shows flexibility of thought. Typical children do this quite naturally. I had a friend whose two-year-old used a clothespin as a pistol, much to her dismay. I immortalized Evan and Glen's similar (though longer awaited) inventiveness in a cartoon.

It is important to start trying to keep autistic children from getting too locked into very rigid patterns of thought early,

Figure 1.10: Brio pistols. Certain toys are very popular with children with autism. Among these are wooden train sets. Most of the time, Evan and Glen liked to put track together and run trains (or, in Glen's case, crash them), but on one occasion, they tried something new.

although this can be difficult. My two were fairly easygoing about using things in unexpected ways, but some children can get quite angry about things that are not as they "should" be. To a large extent, the acceptance of things that are out of place is necessary to the development of a sense of humor. For example, an absurd game called "Is that a hat?" offended Evan at first, but when I kept putting unlikely objects on my head, asking this question and laughing, he finally caught on that it was a joke and started trying to play it himself. Glen was never especially interested in such ridiculous games, and at one point I concluded he didn't have a sense of humor, poor thing. I'm glad I turned out to be wrong.

Glen's commentary

Me? No sense of humor??? This is blatantly wrong and should be deleted from any recent publication that states otherwise.

Mom never stopped me from being obsessed with science fiction elements, and in fact encouraged me to have this interest because it allowed me to become imaginative and allowed me to develop somewhat normally.

As you may know, there are things in life that influence many children, and especially autistic ones. Where do these influences come from? Now, that's a different matter. Most often, these influences come from what a child is most attached to, such as Lego bricks. If the child can imagine a world of his own, he will have no trouble creating an imaginary environment. The picture [Fig. 1:11] will show how attached to a favorite toy one kid can get

Such artistic abilities can be achieved by knowing what such child may like. Lego toys are one such item, although each toy is often part of a selection of the entire Lego system. My favorite Lego sets are those that comprise of Space related groups. These include the original Space, Space Police, Ice Planet 2000, Spyrius, M-Force, Unitron, Explorians, Robo-force, UFO, and more recently, Insectoids. Aqua-Zone also interests me, though I haven't been buying Lego recently with the advent of a cheaper (and more realistic) counterpart, which includes a military variety. Think Lego tanks, frigates, and jet bombers. A child can reenact the entire Gulf War at the flick of a hand!

Figure 1.11: Cape Lego. When Glen was four years old, he helped me build a little town inside a briefcase. He especially liked the rockets and the launch facility. The rocket he is making go "up, up, up" is one he designed himself.

Recently, I have explored the field of "Legomation," pioneered by Colin Williamson, noted for his columns for *PC Gamer*, as well as his unusually violent (for Lego toys, anyway) "Corporal Dan" series. I am, unfortunately, unable to describe Mr.

Williamson's works further, not because of space constraints, but because I have concerns about censorship. It's amazing what you can do with tempura paint these days.

Evan's Commentary:

The *What happened at home?* stories can still be fun to read sometimes.

Fixations: It depends how fixated they are. I was really interested in maps, and my parents got me atlases and maps and globes and...you know. That is sort of encouragement. The fixation changed from maps and things like that to more people and cultures. I'm interested in travel, and I have a collection of foreign coins. These sprang from the interest in geography.

Toys: They are fun. A lot of kids, not necessarily autistic, like construction toys, such as Lego, all of their lives. It's like Roller Coaster Tycoon and Sim City [computer simulation games]. It's fun to build stuff. You can especially see that with me and Roller Coaster Tycoon. It's fun to build and run an amusement park, and see if the rides you build are popular. For a job, I've always wanted to do something in entertainment, like movies, designing rides, music, even culinary arts.

Dramatic play: It's a good thing. Glen acting in that movie definitely sprang from that. It matured as we went along. We just played, and then we had language, and it involved talking.

You're not too old to wear costumes, ever. Some- times you reach an age where you're self-conscious. Like those people at powwows and rendezvous, and it's obvious with actors...it's a way of getting into the role.

The videos: I wanted the camera to make movies. For *The Psychiatrist*, we got some of our inspiration from the Marx brothers, but most of it was just my own creation. I know Glen got a lot of his inspiration from *The Far Side*, Gary Larson cartoon. Glen probably got his accent from

TV or a cartoon somewhere. That would be my guess. Some time ago, we tried to make a second "Psychiatrist," but it sort of fell apart — when I was being the doctor, and Glen was being the patients. He wanted to be the doctor.

Humor and Empathy
Humor

> He that is of merry heart hath a continual feast.
>
> — *Proverbs* 15:15

> The Queen of Hearts
> She bought some parts
> To fix her Chevrolet.
> The Knave of Hearts
> Installed those parts
> And drove the car away.

Glen was not yet six, but he could read very well and was familiar with the original besides, so he knew I was taking liberties with a classic. He was outraged. He did not think it funny at all. In fact, he became quite angry, snatched the book from my grasp and stomped away. A year later, he seemed to find the parody less of a personal affront, but he still didn't like it and he certainly didn't find it amusing.

Unlike Glen, Evan had delighted in song parodies when he was six, although the language of the "Queen of Hearts" would have been too sophisticated for him to understand at that age. His favorite was based on the song from Disney's *Mary Poppins*, "Let's Go Fly a Kite." He and his daddy (who is an inveterate song parodist "because," as he puts it, "I can't remember the real words") had a lot of fun substituting words similar in sound to kite, such as coat or cat. Evan realized these were ridiculous things to go fly, and he laughed delightedly. As he got older, his enjoyment of absurdities grew, and he developed an awareness of puns, even going so far as to compose one of his own when he was barely nine years old:

> Evan: What's the cleanest gene?
>
> Me: I don't know. I don't think the human genome project has found that one yet.
>
> Evan: **Hygiene!**

About then, when Evan was beginning to make up puns and Glen was rejecting the Queen of Hearts' Chevy for the second time, I had the opportunity to meet a young adult with autism. The thing that struck me particularly was his inability to realize I was being facetious when I spoke of "a large statistical sample...of

Figure 1.12: Is that a hat? This was a game that served multiple purposes. I designed it to work on answering yes-no questions. Although it was another three years before Evan could answer yes or no unprompted (i.e., without the questioner following the question with "Say yes or no"), he liked this silly game. Glen did not enjoy this kind of ridiculous play until he was rather older.

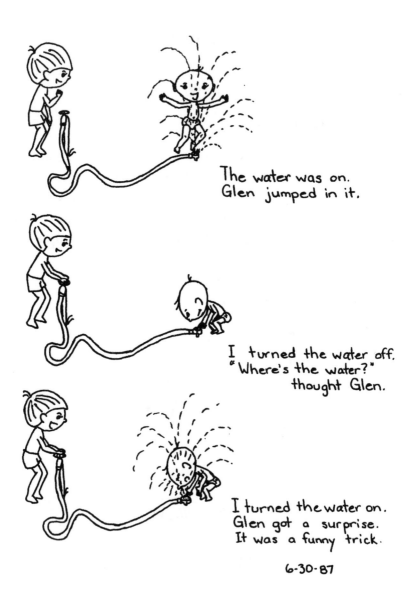

The water was on.
Glen jumped in it.

I turned the water off.
"Where's the water?"
thought Glen.

I turned the water on.
Glen got a surprise.
It was a funny trick.

6-30-87

Figure 1.13: Wet Trick. This shows how important a theory of mind is to a lot of humor. Evan was probably amused then because Glen got blasted with water, but the joke is even funnier to him now that he realizes Glen wasn't expecting it.

two." He gave me the same sort of look Glen had for The Queen of Auto Parts and explained – somewhat scornfully, perhaps – that a population of two could not be considered a large statistical sample. Although I had read that a common deficit of autism is the lack of the ability to understand when people do not mean precisely what they say, until that moment I hadn't considered how great a problem such a seemingly small thing might be.

Prior to this, I had been following the lead of Evan's preschool teacher in using absurdities to teach language, but I hadn't thought much about teaching humor *per se*. So many other things had seemed so much more important. However, once I realized humor is a significant aspect of communication, I began to *explain* why people might find a certain remark or situation funny even before I was sure Evan and Glen knew what I was talking about.

For example, a lot of humor is *connected but unexpected*. It fits the situation in some way but is not at all what is anticipated. The earliest joke enjoyed by most children is the game of peek-a-boo, which is the most fundamental form of something that is *connected* enough not to be startling or even frightening, but *unexpected* enough to be very, very funny. An example of this is "Wet Trick." Evan, anyway, thought it was funny. I don't remember what Glen thought of the joke.

A somewhat more sophisticated device is the list, which is typically a list of items that are connected by type, but of which the final item is unexpected, often because of a disparity in magnitude. Evan made use of this device in his Dreams and Fears paper.

Additionally, our home has all the great humorous literature – cartoon collections of *For Better or Worse*, *Foxtrot*, *Calvin and Hobbes*, *The Far Side*, and *Pogo*. Everybody in the family reads and enjoys the comic strips in the newspaper.

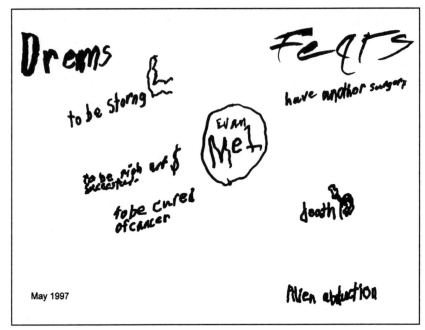

Figure 1.14: Evan's Dreams and Fears. Evan did this as a school assignment in May 1997, when he was fourteen years old. The original paper was 11" x 17". It reads: Drems – to be storng – to be rich and $ successful – to be cured of cancer (Evan Me1) Fears – have another surgery – death – Alien abduction. When I read this the first time, I was very close to crying by the time I got to the final item, and then I laughed aloud.

Humor and absurdity are used extensively by my husband and me both for entertainment and enlightenment. Bad, impromptu puns and absurd malapropisms are common, and Evan particularly enjoys playing with words. Glen is more interested in comics, and his style of humor is strongly influenced by *The Far Side, Calvin and Hobbes* and *Pogo* as well as cartoons on television and the occasional *MAD* Magazine. He also likes *Garfield*, but he's only a kid.

Actually, a lot of children with autism seem to like *Garfield*, possibly because the humor is so physical it is easy to understand even where the words are too sophisticated. When Evan was small, his favorite things on TV were Donald Duck and Chip and Dale cartoons. He didn't laugh, but he watched intently. Because *nobody* can understand Donald Duck or the chipmunks, the humor is very visual, so an almost complete lack of language did not prevent Evan from knowing what was happening.

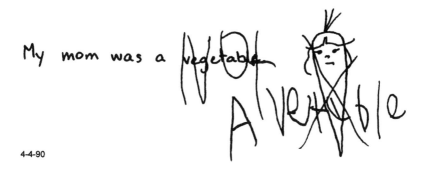

4-4-90

Figure 1.15: Vegetable Mom. It had been a rough day, and Mom certainly felt like a vegetable. Evan was in a grumpy mood, and he took exception to this drawing. He X'ed out the picture and wrote "Not A Vetable" over the parts he found unacceptable. He was seven years old.

Many people with autism can appreciate humor that does not depend on words. Their tendency to take everything literally can make it difficult for them to understand any more sophisticated humor, however. For instance Evan was quite upset by my drawing myself as a vegetable. By then he had developed the means to express his displeasure. Interestingly, he had been quite amused by an earlier cartoon in which I depicted his dad with a green face after riding an amusement park ride. Perhaps Evan could accept a green face because he was aware it was possible, if ridiculous, while he knew Mom could *not* be a vegetable.

It is hard to say how much Evan or Glen understood the humor in my cartoons when I first drew them. I know that by the time they were thirteen and ten respectively, they "got" most of the humor, but they still didn't yet understand why I thought my juggling cartoon was so funny. Four years later, they both laughed delightedly. Their theory of mind is sufficiently mature that they now understand Glen's intention in the cartoon is very different than what Mommy thinks it is.

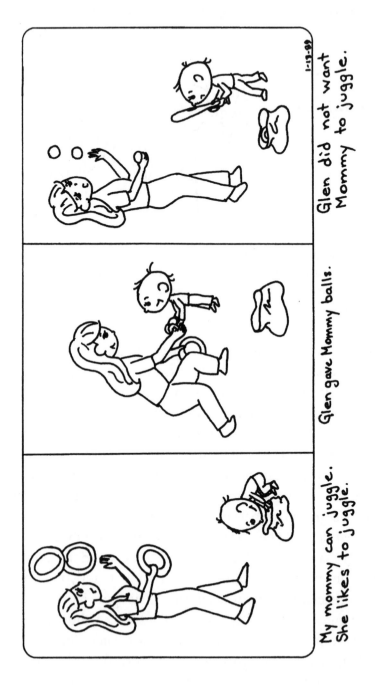

Figure 1.16: The Juggler. This is, more or less, what really happened, although I wasn't actually juggling miscellaneous toys at first. I was juggling rings at first, but I decided they would take longer to draw and be distracting. Glen brought me my set of balls, and I had gotten going very nicely by the time he returned with the baseball bat.

As for Glen, after discovering Shel Silverstein's poetry for children (and *MAD* Magazine), he actually laughed at my rendition of the Queen of Hearts. Once. But by then, he was eleven and claimed to be too old for such things.

Glen's Commentary

I actually did like the Queen of Auto Parts after laughing once, but I didn't show it.

Glen's Strip: These strips prove a point: when humor and autism collide, the result is a look at what reality should be like. Take for example a kid who loves bombs and explosions. He also might like exaggerated body/facial features, to make characters seem really funny. So he might decide to draw it in strip form. Combined with a look at himself, a knack at drawing backgrounds, and an assortment of funny characters, and he might get something like this [Figure 1.17].

Evan's Commentary

Hygiene pun: We were watching a program on genetics, and the gene pun just came to me.

I thought puns were very funny, and I still sort of do, even when people go, "Oh...kaay." It's also easy to make up puns.

Hopes and Fears: I was being facetious about the alien abduction part. A lot of my humor is facetious, but I'm not facetious about my humor.

Mom the Vegetable: I was probably taking it literally.

Feelings and Empathy

Tact is after all a kind of mind-reading.

— Sarah Orne Jewett, 1896

Empathy is an area of significant weakness for anybody in the autism spectrum. It's more fundamental than simply not being

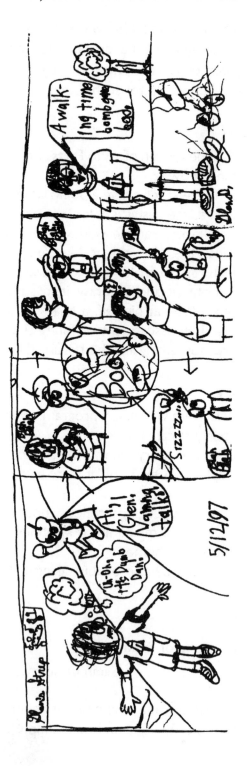

Figure 1.17: Glen's Strip: This strip is a throwback to an earlier comic strip I did: "Dumb Dan." Most of the Dumb Dan comic strips featured cartoon violence, and certainly an awful lot of gags. Of course, I got tired of doing them and opted for something else. He does pop in elsewhere sometimes, and usually goes out with a bang...often quite literally.

able to read facial expression – although that common skill deficit doesn't make it any easier. For someone with autism, the ability to experience the feelings of another can be as mystical – and seem as mythical – as an ability to read minds.

Most children learn empathy the way they learn language. Their brains are wired for it, and the normal experiences of childhood are sufficient instruction for them to attain a reasonable mastery. But in the same way autistic children need to be taught language systematically, they also need to be taught empathy.

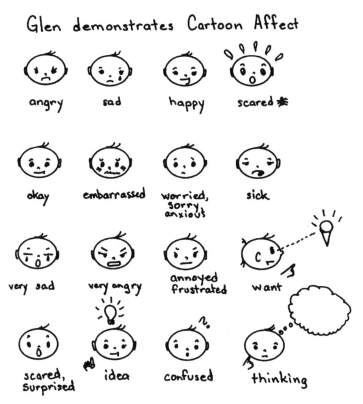

Figure 1.18: Glen demonstrates Cartoon Affect. I drew these expressions using Glen's face because his two hairs are faster to draw than the bowl-cut Evan sports, but it is also something of a reflection of real life. Evan has very low affect. He will smile for a camera, chuckle when amused, or very occasionally cry when distressed, but otherwise he exhibits little facial expression.

I did not consciously set out to instill empathy in my children. Many of the recent books on the subject, such as *Emotional Intelligence* by Daniel Goleman or *Mindreading* by Sanjida O'Connor, had not yet been written. The books I had read spoke little, if at all, of empathy. On the other hand, *How to Talk So Kids*

Evan climbed up.

He fell down.

It hurt.
Evan cried.

4-14-87

Figure 1.19: Evan's Accident. This is one of the earliest What happened at home? *cartoons. It wasn't long after this that the teacher advised the parents to write the stories from the child's point of view, but originally I wrote this in third person. This mishap must have hurt Evan a lot, so it was an excellent lesson, both in language and feelings.*

Will Listen and Listen So Kids Will Talk by Adele Faber and Elaine Mazlish emphasized the validation of children's feelings as a way to encourage communication. Their ideas made (and still make) a lot of sense to me.

I'm not sure I realized that my sons had very little understanding of their own emotional states, but I did know they didn't have the language to describe them. Before I could get my kids to either listen or talk, I had to teach them the words.

I began by using the *What happened at home?* cartoons which we were already using for language instruction to help Evan give names to his own feelings. As always, I kept the language simple and the emotions few. I wrote about happy, sad, scared, hurt, liking (and not liking), and mad (angry). I used the same word every time I described a feeling, even if the intensity of the emotion varied.

One of the first cartoons I drew happened to depict Evan getting hurt. He gave me several more opportunities for reminding him about "hurt" by stubbing his toe, stepping barefoot on a Lego brick, stepping barefoot on a bee, and so on. Then I put Glen into the picture.

Glen was normally pretty unresponsive to pain, but on one occasion Evan hurt him badly enough that Glen cried. While (as I look at it now) the cartoon might seem to depict a cause-and-effect relationship between Evan's accident and Glen's drumming on Evan's head, in reality there was none. Drumming has always been one of Glen's stims, and he happened to like the feel of thumping people on the head regardless of whether his subject cared for it or not. Glen was not "getting even" with his brother, he was just doing something he enjoyed doing.

Although I wrote the cartoons from Evan's point of view, Glen liked to look at them too. When I wrote "My Space Adventure" story for Evan (Figure 1.4), it was Glen who read, "Up, up, up." (He pronounced it "puh, puh, puh.") I believe both children learned not only about their own feelings but began to under-

Figure 1.20: Hurt. Evan knew about "hurt" when he felt it. He needed to know he can hurt other people, too. Note that the drawings depict the actions in the same order, left to right, as the words that describe them.

stand about others' feelings as well. These are the first two steps in acquiring empathy.

I'd like to say my cartoon caused Glen to stop thumping people on the head, but it was a while before we were able to convince him that it hurt the person he thumped and therefore he shouldn't do it. He still drums on my back and shoulders (sometimes surprising me with a sudden onslaught) but he has learned to temper it so it doesn't hurt. Usually. And when I tell him he's hurting me, he stops.

Even typical children may not know that their own actions can hurt others unless someone tells them. Due to theory of mind deficits, autistic children have significantly more difficulty learning this information even when told. Unfortunately, many people do not realize they need to *tell* their children something that seems so obvious.

I once met a mother who was concerned because her child had the habit of poking other children in the eye, and she wondered why he liked to hurt them. Since he was five years old and autistic, it's a pretty safe bet he didn't *know* he was hurting them. He was either oblivious to their reaction and intrigued by something about their eyes, or he enjoyed the reaction he got without understanding any of the emotional content driving that reaction. It had never occurred to the mother that her child didn't realize he was hurting anyone.

One autistic boy I know has been disciplined chiefly with rules, punishments and rewards. No one is in the habit of explaining the effects his actions have on others. For example, if he were to hit another child, he would not be told he shouldn't do

Figure 1.21: Evan and Glen help. They were totally unaware Mommy didn't feel good.

it because it *hurt* the other child. Instead, he would be told it was against the social rules and that he would lose privileges should he do it again. If he could keep from breaking the social rules, he would get something he wanted. He still has very little empathy. At thirteen, he laughingly told his mother about an administrator at his school. "Mr Smith is so funny! When he gets mad, his face gets red, and the veins stand out on his neck!" The boy's enjoyment of the display was not marred by any real awareness of the man's emotion.

Our mommy wanted to sleep.

She did not want to play.

7-16-88

Figure 1.27: Mommy doesn't want to play. They still didn't understand that Mommy wasn't well, but they did know it was unusual for her to lie down in the middle of the day.

It is true that appealing to empathy is a poor disciplinary tool for children who have none. But even if there's no evident short-term payoff, instruction in consideration for others' feelings should be a part of any discipline program. Empathy can eventually play an important role in the development of self-discipline as well as forming the basis for social understanding.

Figure1.23: Presents make Mommy feel better. At the time I drew this cartoon, both kids assumed I was well because I got up. Not quite six years later, they were able to look at the cartoon and realize I hadn't really felt better. They also laughed about their choices for get-well presents.

I have a very telling set of three cartoons that document the beginnings of empathy in Evan and Glen. Each one shows what the two of them did when their mother was ill. In the first, they took advantage of my indisposition to make a mess. Evan was four, while Glen wasn't yet two. A year later, although their reaction to the problem was not in the least empathetic, they at least showed an awareness there was something wrong. This was a step in the right direction.

By the time Evan was seven and Glen was almost five, they had begun to discover empathy. In the final cartoon of the series, they showed they were not only aware I wasn't feeling good, they tried to do something to make me feel better. They brought me presents. Glen drew a stack of cartoons depicting a stick figure in bed, while Evan brought me one of my own barrettes and some hairpins. I think it was Glen who supplied the books – a couple of stories for beginning readers and a book on breastfeeding. Except for the cartoons, they were singularly inappropriate gifts, but I was thrilled to have this evidence that they cared about how I felt.

Glen's Commentary

I don't know if I have any true empathy yet. It's a relatively new concept to me, so I'm not too sure. Although I seem to display that kind of a trait, trying to get people to try something only based on my own experience. For example, I at one point tried to get my friend Josh to try a computer game I liked. However, he insisted that he would not like the game, despite substantial evidence it was a good game, so after several tries I eventually gave up. Then I introduced him to another game I like, and he *loved* it. I'm still trying to figure out why he didn't like the first one as much as the second one, even though the first one has a better story. I can only figure out two reasons: 1) the second game has more replay value and 2) he values the gameplay itself rather than focusing on the story.

Evan's Commentary

If someone I know got hurt, I would say something like, "Are you okay?" And I would feel bad. On the way home from camp a few years ago, one of my friends got sick and I cried about it. I think maybe I overreacted, but I felt bad.

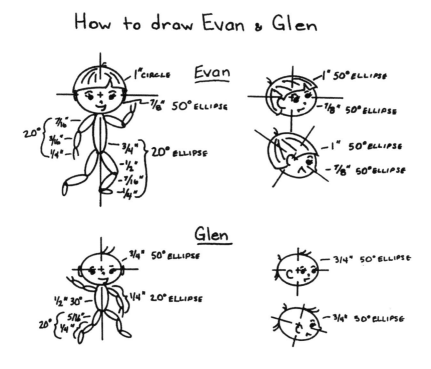

Figure 1.24: How to Draw Evan and Glen. Evan and Glen are made up of overlapping ellipses as shown. I have no idea where I came up with the style of drawing the mouth, but for the bodies I recalled a book about drawing the human figure I read when I was a child. Ths artist used ellipses to rough in the shape, although I don't think he (or she) used an ellipse template.

The Evan and Glen Cartoons

I pretty much stopped drawing the "Evan and Glen" cartoons when Evan was seven-and-a-half and Glen was five. This was partly because I had been doing them for over three years and was getting pretty burned out, but mostly it was because I hardly ever needed to communicate that way any more. I still threw together a quick story on occasion, but most of the time I could convey what I needed to by talking or writing a simple note. As for the lessons contained in the pages and pages of cartoons I had already done, they were still available. Periodically, Evan and Glen would spread out the notebooks and read, reminisce and chuckle.

I am not an artist, and I'm not really even a cartoonist, but I am an engineer. I devised a very mechanical, reasonably repeatable method for drawing cartoon characters to represent members of my family. Drawing objects is easier than drawing people for me, but I can certainly find examples in Evan's language books where a picture looks only vaguely like the object it represented. The idea here wasn't perfection but recognizability.

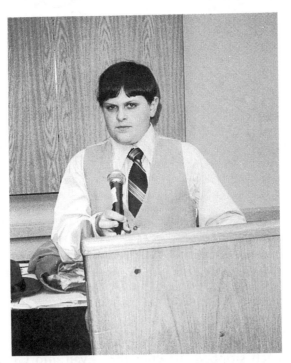

Figure 1.25: Glen at Palm Springs. Glen was eleven years old, and he felt no anxiety about addressing an auditorium full of adults. He insisted on wearing a suit for the occasion, so his dad lent him an old corduroy three-piece suit (which fit Glen very nicely). Glen has since overcome his fears both of Lola Bunny and of pictures of nude women. Fortunately, the idea of actual nudity still makes him nervous.

Drawing cartoons – or picture stories – is a fair amount of work, but I know the ones I did for Evan and Glen still mean a lot to them. I consider my Glen and Evan cartoons some of the best things I have ever done, in spite of the fact they are not especially great work. I believe the cartoons were instrumental in promoting not only the language development originally intended, but imagination, humor and empathy as well. Having these traits does not magically turn Evan and Glen into typical kids, but that was never my goal. I wanted them to be happy...and they are. When they aren't, they can make a joke about it and go on.

Where I get my ideas

by Glen Darlington
March 31, 1997
Presented April 6, 1997
at the California State Speech, Language and
Hearing Professionals Conference
in Palm Springs, CA.

- I get my various ideas from movies, mind quirks and so on.

- These ideas can spark weird dreams.

- Sometimes I see nude women in my dreams. One example of a dream I've had is the first time I saw nudity in my own dreams. It turns out I was riding a truck toward a museum of science, history, math, archaeology and all that stuff we know currently. When I got into the museum lobby I saw a TV screen showing a naked woman wearing spandex underwear (no other clothing than that!). What was more surprising was it was actually happening. The most surprising thing was she was a registered Warner Brothers' character (Hello Nurse from *Animaniacs*, a well-known kids' show on WB Channel 5). About a few seconds later, I was walking by some display cases with some weird things. Suddenly, I fell into a display case about vintage teddy bears, and while I was falling, I saw parts of the Phonecian alphabet on a chart. I think this was from reading "History of the Universe," which had small stints of nudity and Tantristic acts.[1] There was even Xerxes dallying with an officer's wife in there. I think it is a little embarrassing to talk about sex in this meeting, but I think it is necessary to explain why I've gotten nude women in my dreams in the last few months. Actually, there were only two nude women.

- But all kidding aside, the second time I saw a nude woman, it was this black, or rather African-American woman in a music video. Must have been around her twenties or something. Shortly afterwards, I saw a book sort of format, and suddenly there was this tall silhouette standing in front of me. To my surprise, it was Bugs Bunny, another well-known cartoon character – one of the most popular this era has ever seen. He was giving me a little pep talk, talking about all this gibberish. I don't know what he was talking about. The details are a bit sketchy. So he ran back to his hole and jumped into it. That's all I remember about the dream, except soon I was yelling, "Bugs! Bugs! Where are you?"

- And now, another involvement with Warner Brothers characters was with a single and rather female-human…actually, it was Lola Bunny,[2] three duplicates that had gone totally wrong. Something about their DNA structures was a bit different. For those who don't know who Lola Bunny is, she is the newest Loony Tunes character, from Space Jam. The first time I encountered two of the three duplicates was on a TV show with Bugs Bunny, and the guest star, amazingly enough, was a well-known Disney character, Donald Duck, famous for his insatiable temper. Of course, this was an older version of Donald Duck, not quite as advanced. You could actually see little balls on his knees, rather ball-shaped knees. Well, anyway, after the TV show was finished, I saw Bugs Bunny and those two slightly different duplicates of Lola Bunny in a Jacuzzi. I said "Hi," to them, and then I stood in front of school on a little stage, and I think were acting out a little play…but I don't really have

---

1   A phrase Glen *invented*, meaning: sex acts, derived from Tantrism, a Hindu Yoga (practice) celebrating sex. Tantrism was mentioned in *Cartoon History of the Universe* by Larry Gonick.

2   Lola Bunny scared Glen. She had the caricatured head, cottontail and feet of a rabbit but was otherwise built like a well-endowed human female.

enough time, so I think I'll go on to the next encounter, this time with the third duplicate.

- The third duplicate that I encountered in my dreams was actually similar to Lola Bunny, but the suit of clothes were wrong. She was wearing white high-heels and a white dress. The details are a bit sketchy. The dream starts in a little, lonely diner. This little, squat lady with sort of the features of Sniz and Fondue of Kablam,[3] except she was a lady, and she was wearing retro, twenties-style clothes, or more like nineteen-hundreds. One reason I knew this was she was black and white; another reason was her clothing was out of style. Whenever she took a step, she sort of went, BOOM! BOOM! BOOM! Then, I tasted some cookie dough — it was regular sort of sugary cookie dough with chocolate chips in it. I also saw the old Bugs Bunny and this cannon guy on a pirate ship. Soon, me and my mom were driving down a Hollywood Boulevard that looked kind of like the Golden Gate Bridge! Except the bridge part said, "Hollywood Boulevard." Then we went to this little store with a clown's head at the end of it. We drove straight through the store (we never knocked the front door down, because for some reason there wasn't any door). Then we parked near the cereal section of the store. Then I checked out the store, the book section, and then I saw these two pink doors, each one marked with white or some certain color. Suddenly these two frogmen appeared, and I decided to go with them through the doors. A short, squat frogman went into one door, while me and the taller frogman went into the other. We sat down, and I was reading this paper with all of these cartoon characters very similar to those of Disney and Warner Brothers caliber cartoon characters, while the other frogman sitting next to me was talking about Allie Alligator. I think it was some sort of horoscope. Then I heard a female voice saying, "Hello, you big hunk of a man." Then the frogman, fearing what might happen, jumped out of his seat and started trying to break down one of the walls by the stairway. I was shouting, "Don't break that wall down; go to the stairway, it's your only chance!" And then, when she was coming

---

3   Kablam was a short-lived animated television series. Sniz and Fondue were a couple of rather unattractive characters in the show.

down, she was talking about this stuff, I think it was gambling numbers, and I was yelling, "Too late! Too late!" Then the frogman broke through the wall, and I think he got teleported somewhere else, probably to the crates around the doors. She was coming towards me, so I jumped out of my seat, and ran towards the door and broke it down. Then, I stopped. Then I turned around towards her, pulling out this little thing. I couldn't tell if it was a small handgun, a lightswitch or part of a water faucet. Then I yelled "Dip gun!" And then she said, "No, you don't," in a feminine voice. I also said, "Don't vorry, I von't!" in a German sort of accent. Then I turned around again, put the thing in my pocket (whatever it was) and started running and jumping over the crates. The tall frogman and the small frogman accompanied me in the chase. Then that part of the dream ended, and then I saw a sequnece in which a refurbished Mom was holding and waving and stretching green socks in front of my face in my own bedroom. And that was where the dream ended.

- Of course, after this dream happened, I imagined another sort of ending, this time involving characters from a well-known Lucas Arts computer game and a character in a Sega Saturn video game. It all starts when we are running around the crates, the female, or rather, duplicate of Lola Bunny's face starts turning red. She starts fuming red gases, and suddenly fireballs start shooting out from where she is. The forces of Hell are against us. It is sort of a DOOM situation. Then the frogmen get engulfed in flames and become demons. Then I jump into the car and I drive it, trying to avoid the fireballs coming out the clown's mouth. Then one hits, and I have to jump out of the car before the car bursts into flame. I jump out in good enough time to get close enough....

When it is pointed out to Glen that most people do the opposite, think up happy endings to nightmares instead of nightmare endings to silly dreams, he points out this is exciting, and having a female in his dream is a nightmare.

References

Charman, T. and Baron-Cohen, S. (1997) Brief Report: Prompted Pretend Play in Autism. *Journal of Autism and Developmental Disorders 27*, 325–332.

Faber, A. and Mazlish, E. (1982) *How to Talk so Kids will Listen and Listen so Kids will Talk.* New York: Avon Books

Frith, U. (1989) *Autism: Explaining the Enigma.* Cambridge, MA: Basil Blackwell Inc.

Goleman, D. (1995) *Emotional Intelligence.* New York: Bantam Books.

Lansky, B. (1986) *Baby Talk.* Deephaven, MN: Meadowbrook Inc.

O'Connel, S. (1997) *Mindreading: An Investigation into How We Learn to Love and Lie.* New York: Doubleday.

St. James, P.J. and Tager-Flusberg, M. (1994) An Observational Study of Humor in Autism and Down Syndrome. *Journal of Autism and Developmental Disorders 24*, 603–617.

Simons, J. and Oishi, S. (1987) *The Hidden Child.* Rockville, MD: Woodbine House.

Walker, M. (1975) *Backstage at the Strips.* New York: Mason/Charter.

Wing, L. (1972) *Autistic Children.* Secaucus, NJ: Citadel Press.

2

The Myth of Social Skills

Linda Andron

One of many lessons I have learned along this journey is the myth of social skills. Since the primary challenge these children face is social interaction, all those who love and work with them have sought to find a set of rules we can teach them that will allow them to function "normally." The agencies who serve them are forever looking for a pre-packaged program that can teach these skills in a 12–16 week format.

First we must ask, what is a social skill? Are we referring to the rules of social interaction? What are these rules? Do they remain constant from setting to setting? Children with High Functioning Autism (HFA) and AS love rules. If you can give them a rule that makes sense, they will follow it without deviation. So it should be simple to teach social rules. Let's start with a simple and seemingly obvious one: saying please and thankyou. The kids understand that they need to say please to get something that they want. But since they are such literal thinkers they assume that whenever they say please it should lead to them getting what they asked for. This leads to begging and has led to many a tantrum when the rule they see as infallible is not followed. Most of the children get the idea that they need to say thankyou for things they are given. However, it is more difficult to understand the rule when it does not apply to something concrete. Guthrie, for example, who could not thank his aunt until he knew what he was thankful for. Difficulties with understanding that people do not know what they are thinking lead to occasions where they just assume the other person knows they are thankful. One adult commented that when he went to visit a friend's factory, his sister reminded him to say thankyou. He said that he needed to remind himself that people do not know that you are thankful unless you say so. Nor do they always understand why they are being thanked. When Ruth thanked Josh for going somewhere with her, he said he didn't know why she was thanking him since it had not been his idea. Thus, it is clear that we cannot just teach these children a rule, but must always keep in mind how they see the world and give them the "theory" behind the rule, as well as exceptions to it.

Victor was an example of a child who really wanted to interact and was hungry for rules he could follow that would allow him to do so. One day he wanted to play with a toy that another child had brought to group. He began the litany of "skills" he had been taught in many settings. After being rejected repeatedly, he hauled off and socked the other kid. He then turned to staff and said, "You failed me." The message was, I followed "your" rules and they didn't work.

The tendency to see the parts without understanding the whole has been deemed the theory of central coherence by Uta Frith (1989). Central coherence is described as the tendency to draw together diverse information to construct higher meaning in context. Thus, in those with neuro-typical information processing, there is a tendency to make sense of situations using the context. Those with autism and AS do not. This leads to insistence on sameness and routine, attention to detail, and obsessional preoccupations. This is the reason that these children crave rules that they can understand and that will help them predict. However, because they cannot see the situation in context we run the risk of them misapplying the rules and looking even more odd because of this. The children who learn the skill of "greeting" appropriately are a prime example. The rule is say "hello" when you come in and "good-bye" when you leave.

What happens is that they develop a routine that requires them to say hello and good-bye to each individual in the room, without getting the contextual cue that a "good-bye everyone" would be more appropriate. Many children who have come from structured behavioral programs learn to greet and introduce themselves in a rote manner. Every time they enter a room they walk up to each child and say, "Hello, my name is...", even if they have played with the same child week after week. I also well remember our efforts to teach the children the "skills" required to ask to enter a game. We practiced and practiced. What we forgot was to tell them to read the context. Sometimes the situation demands that you just wait in line. So when Joey put his carefully practiced skills into play, he was laughed at by the other kids, who said "No, you can't play, go wait in line like everyone else."

Social scripting would seem a good way to teach specific interactions. It is even more specific than a rule which has to be applied. But again the lack of ability to see the whole must be taken into account. Witness the story of an 11-year-old who had been presented with a social script for appropriate introductions. At his sixth grade orientation, he went to his new teacher and said, "Hello my name is Patrick. I am pleased to meet you and look forward to being in your class." At first glance, this would seem to represent a child with good social skills. But instead his mother correctly interpreted that he had doomed himself socially. The teacher just thought he was foreign, but the other kids saw him as a "dork." During a class at a residential camp, Alexis was listening to the teacher, raising her hand and waiting to be called on. Her behavior specialist was impressed with her excellent social skills. The other kids, however, were giggling and giving each other messages. Again, instead of helping her to fit in, good "social skills" were leading to social isolation.

We have been caught unawares by this tendency to see the parts without the whole. On one occasion, we were using an excellent video curriculum that demonstrates how to handle anger. Following watching one of the modules focusing on how to handle people who are angry with you, the children went outside to play. Katie, a child who had rarely shown any aggression, began to pick fights. When asked what she was doing she said that she was getting people angry at her so that she could practice dealing with their anger.

Problems with weak central coherence also affect the children's ability to be empathetic. Glen clearly has empathetic feelings for Josh's mother. He would not want to hurt her feelings. Yet, because of his focus on detail it is very hard to him for see how things affect her and the rest of the family. Ruth is well aware that Glen only eats white food. To this end, she prepared white corn, mashed potatoes and turkey. Glen, however, was unable to eat this meal because turkey is only for Thanksgiving.

Remember Josh has a rule about being nice to people's parents (see Chapter 3). This would seem to be an excellent social rule. It shows his ability to observe a situation. At first glance, it seems like he has used good theory of mind as well as demonstrated central coherence. It shows that he understands the perspective of the other. In fact, he has missed a small but important detail that was pointed up to him by his neuro-typical twin. This involved the perspective of the other child, i.e., if you are too nice to someone else's parents they will think you are a dork. Temple Grandin has given us much insight into the need for scientific observation to learn social mores and emotions. She has referred to herself as "an anthropologist on Mars" (Sacks 1995). Many adults we have seen confirm this experience. Those who do best are often thought to be foreign. They figure out what to do, but it is a little stilted.

What about conversational rules? A central one would be turn taking. This would seem to mean waiting for one person to finish before beginning to speak. i.e. don't interrupt. How could that backfire? Well, if they are holding forth on a subject, you are breaking a rule by interrupting them. Also, they focus on the detail of saying "excuse me" and, without getting the context, feel that the listener must immediately attend to them. Also, for those who can read the context, there are, indeed, places where people interrupt to enter a conversation. Another conversational rule is referencing. This means that you must give the other person enough information to know what you are speaking about. But if you believe that everyone already knows what you are thinking, it is hard to remember to do this.

Another "skill" deemed critical is that of eye contact. We must remember that in some cultures eye contact is actually seen as rude. Moreover, it is equally important to break eye contact intermittently, so that the other person does not think that you are staring. However, there are no specific rules we can teach for when this should happen. Many of the adults we have worked with have faced serious consequences when people felt that their "staring" was tantamount to stalking. It is far better to teach the concept of shared attention (Sigman and Capps 1997). Thus, the goal is to help the children learn to look at what they or the other person are talking about. Also, we counsel them to let others know that it is hard for them to look at them and that they are not trying to be rude.

Part of the diagnostic picture of these children is that they do not demonstrate social and emotional reciprocity. It has been our experience that these children are very empathic with each other, particularly in regard to experiences they have shared, such as being teased. It would appear that they care a great deal about others, but miss the mark as to what the other might be experiencing. Glen's question to Josh's mother about whether she had started menopause was, in fact, very empathic (see Chapter 3). He knew that women in menopause had hot flashes and had figured that that evening's cool weather would be helpful. Again, he missed the context and had to be told that this would not be an appropriate topic to bring up with others. When the author's husband passed away, Brian said, "It must have been awful for you the first time you opened the front door and realized that your husband wasn't there." This was, perhaps, the most "right on" comment anyone had made. He picked a very salient detail. But, again, missing the context, he went on to ask many inappropriate questions about the details of the death. He could imagine what it would be like to come back to an empty house, but not comprehend what it would be like to relive someone's death.

The social rule that you must tell the truth makes a great deal of sense to the kids. But this gets them into an incredible amount of trouble. They tell people that they are ugly, have gained weight, have bad breath, or that their hair is getting gray. The concept of telling a "white lie" to avoid hurting someone's feelings is totally foreign to them. Chris came to the graduation party for one of our staff. He tasted chips made from pitta bread and declared them awful. When he found out they had been made by the woman's grandmother who had gone to a lot of trouble to do something nice, he replied, "Then I guess she is just a terrible cook." In general, they have trouble accepting that people say things that they don't really mean. Thus, when the principal asked James how many more detentions he thought he would have that semester, he assumed that he was supposed to answer the question. When he calculated and came up with a number, he was seen as being rude, yet again. Many of the children with Asperger Syndrome are initially referred because they are rude to teachers. This often consists of correcting a teacher in front of the other children. When we try to explain how this might make the teacher feel, they often answer that it is their responsibility to make sure the children get the true facts, and one youngster once added that if the teacher did not know the right answer she should not be teaching.

So, if we can't teach a list of rules or skills that will help children fit in, what can we do? First, we must always be aware of the issues related to theory of mind and weak central coherence. We must always help them to understand the cause and effect of situations. We must always explain the reasons behind what we are asking them to do. We must always help them to understand the "theory" behind what we are requesting. We need to make use of their strength in scientific inquiry, but then help them see where there are flaws in their conclusions. We must always help them to see the whole that is the result of the parts. This is best done in naturalistic settings, where they can experience various situations and observe the results of their actions. We must help them learn to manage their anxieties. Often they have the cognitive knowledge of what to do, but are paralyzed in the situation.

Many of the difficulties with social interaction that the children experience seem to be because of anxiety and motor planning. We have repeatedly seen evidence that the children do learn certain appropriate rules in an intellectual way. They can sit in circle time at group meetings and identify what should be done in various situations. One method we found successful is to have the staff portray the wrong way to do something and let the kids correct it. This gives them a sense of success and completion. However, when a similar situation occurs in free play they are not able to put these "skills" into practice. When asked why, they often say that they are too scared to think or that they couldn't stop their bodies. This is why social interaction needs to be taught in naturalistic settings that allow for immediate feedback or videotaping. We have found that unless they can see the situation they cannot relate to it. One day Michael was harassing his sister. His mother asked him how he would feel if she was harassing him. His answer: "I don't know, it isn't happening right now."

In social interaction, timing is everything. Auditory processing and motor planning difficulties will make it hard for children to respond quickly enough for smooth social interaction. This is another area where understanding the differences and being able to explain them to others is critical. Also, since many of the children are such perfectionists it is important to show them that it is okay to make mistakes. Bob was terrified to make a decision for fear that he would make the wrong one. This makes friendship difficult. Again, he needed to learn how this made the other person feel.

It must be said that occasionally situation-specific rules may be helpful. Bob used to laugh when he thought about people in his neighborhood. When others asked him what was funny, he would relate some very mundane experience such as watching his neighbor fix his car. When he began attending a magnet school, we were concerned that his laughter might be misinterpreted by others on the bus. He was able to understand that others, particularly minority groups, might think that he was laughing at them. He decided that the best rule was just to not laugh on the bus at all. This stood him in good stead. He did not have to judge the context to see which rule to follow. The rule was black and white and thus comfortable. When he started to drive, he asked whether we thought it would be okay for him to laugh in his car. He thought about it himself and decided that someone might think he was laughing at them and pull a gun on him. So no laughing in the car either.

An emphasis on teaching "friendship" skills, rather than social skills, may be helpful. Tony Attwood has delineated these as:

- Entering – how the child joins a group of children and responds to the welcome they are offering.

- Assistance – recognizing when and how to provide assistance to others as well as seeking assistance from others.

- Compliments – knowing how to both give and receive.

- Criticism – knowing when criticism is appropriate and how to tolerate it.

- Accepting Suggestions – incorporating the ideas of others into an activity.

- Reciprocity and Sharing – sharing of conversation, direction of an activity and resources.

- Conflict Resolution – managing disagreement with compromise and recognizing the opinions of others.

- Monitoring and Listening – regularly observing the other person to monitor their contribution to the activity and body language. Using their own body language to show interest in the other person.

- Empathy – recognizing when appropriate comments and actions are required in response to the other person's circumstances and the positive and negative feelings of others.

- Avoiding and Ending – the appropriate behavior and comments to maintain solitude and end the interaction. (Attwood 2000)

We must help these children to learn to recognize their own emotions. It is not possible to empathize with the emotions of others if you do not recognize or cannot deal with your own. In the name of behavior management, their expression of emotion has often been severely curtailed. And we have found that they well remember the experience. When he was in his early twenties, Sam recalled an incident that occurred when he was three and on the unit at UCLA. He recalls trying to speak and not being understood. The result was a tantrum that put him in time out. His conclusion was that he was not supposed to speak. When asked how he had learned to speak, he said that one of the staff "came into my world and got me. She did this by sitting beside me and swinging her leg like I was." This he interpreted to mean that what he was doing was acceptable.

How do we teach emotions? There has been a great emphasis on teaching people to recognize facial expressions. This is important, but can backfire if only done in a cognitive format. The children often become very adept at recognizing the nuances. The problem for the younger children is that they often come to believe that if they can make the person's face look a certain way the feeling will follow. So they will go up to their mother and turn up the corners of her mouth to make her happy. Or they make an exaggerated face and expect you to know why they are angry. Again the problem with central coherence comes in. We have shown the teenagers soap operas with the sound off and asked them to tell how the actors are feeling from their body language and facial expression. They are amazingly adept at this. They tell us that the problem is when the words and the facial expression and body language don't match. They can see the parts, but again, they cannot integrate the whole. As part of the Asperger's Diagnostic Checklist, children are asked to demonstrate faces for emotions, including happy, sad, angry, scared, surprised, bored, embarrassed, and proud. One of the evaluation parameters is the speed with which they are able to do this. Sometimes there is a clear delay that may be the result of the need to cognitively process what the face looks like. Sometimes you can see a child compose the face, piece by piece (Attwood 1998).

It is important for the child to see his own face when he is experiencing an emotion. This can be done by showing their face in the mirror, taking pictures or, perhaps best, with video. Children with autism and AS have trouble experiencing themselves in a situation. They remember all the details of the event, but do not see themselves as part of it. It is important to help them understand the cause and effect in situations and to learn to verbalize the emotions they are feeling. This is often very difficult. Comic Strip Conversations (Gray 1994) can be used to help the child tell you what they are thinking. This may help them to make the connection with an emotion. It is also important the parents and others label their own emotions for children and explain to them the reason that they are feeling that way. It is also important to check their understanding of situations where people are being facetious.

Many people advocate the need for children with HFA and AS to be exposed to as many normal peers as possible. At first glance, this would be the best way for them to learn to socialize. But remember that they tend to focus on details and miss the gestalt. So without a guide, they may pick up and exaggerate the wrong details. If they observe for a long while, they can usually figure it out, but by that time the gestalt has changed. When I speak to classes where children with HFA and AS are included, I ask the foreign born children what it was like for them to learn our culture. They quickly indicate how difficult it was. I then suggest the analogy that, for kids with HFA and AS, it is like they are moving into a new country every day.

Because these kids do not look disabled, it is hard for others to understand their behavior. One of the things that we can do is to help the children understand and value their difference and then educate others. This is the message of Max and Jennifer's chapter and the monologues of Chris, Glen, and Alexis (see Appendix). This also applies to specific differences that children have. Alan had learned that he could not always win a game, but he liked to complete the game even if he lost. This would have caused a problem if he waited to say something until the other child had won. However, we found that if he explained it to the other child ahead of time, it did not pose a problem.

We have found that neuro-typical children are usually happy to have the children share their special skills with them. Pokemon has been a great boon to the socialization of kids with HFA and AS. Because of their great memory for detail they are able to help other children get through various levels. For once being obsessed with something is socially appropriate.

However, we must always emphasize the importance of understanding the other child's perspective. The children in James' after-school program were excited when they realized that he could read the rules of a game to them. At first, they were also happy when he showed them the correct moves in checkers. Ultimately, they told him that it was okay if they made a mistake and did not want him to tell them where to move. Here again was another example of attention to detail leading to inflexible adherence to rules. It took several Social Stories (Gray 2000) to help James understand the other children's perspective.

Perhaps the most critical variable in interaction is the desire for it. Many children with HFA and AS are perfectly content to be on their own. Several children have told us that they are alone but not lonely. I often tell them what a valuable skill it is to be on your own. Many neuro-typical kids get drawn into gangs and drugs out of a desperate need to belong. But we must also help the children see the value of being with others. We tell them that it is our job to help them learn how to be with others and that it is their decision whether they want to be. Even if they don't want to socialize, they will need to learn to be with others, as they will need to deal with them in their adult careers. Brad did not see the importance of greeting people. However, when we explained to him that to be a world-famous zoologist, he would need to greet people, make small talk, and give compliments, he quickly learned to do so. In order to learn to be with people, you must be with people.

Sometimes the children are motivated to interact and are able to connect, but often with other marginal children. When Bob began attending the magnet school, he was almost immediately accepted by a group of marginal kids, who often got in trouble. As he put it, he was the only one in the group who got E's on his report card. It was very important for him to follow school rules, but he had learned that friendship skills dictated that you did not tattle on friends. This was a subject that bothered Bob a great deal and he brought it up for group discussion on many occasions. He finally found a way to tell the principal about tagging and other activities without his friends (or their huge brothers) finding out. When his friend brought a snake to school, he was able to tell him that he was uncomfortable knowing that he was breaking a rule. Other kids have had trouble resisting peer pressure and have literally been caught "holding the bag" for drug dealers. Not knowing how to judge character, they have believed that these people were their friends.

Most of the children do want to have friends. They may still need their solitude, but are happy to share it with a friend. We cannot stress enough the importance of friendships. In his doctoral dissertation, Christopher Craig studied the factors that affect the quality of life for adults with HFA, from the perspective of the adults themselves. The results indicated that only one variable – "hours spent with friends" – was able to significantly predict scores on any of the quality of life measures. Yet, such emphasis is put on having "normal friends" that the children often become isolated and never get to practice being with a friend. We must ask ourselves who we choose as friends. It is usually people who share our interests. Why not the same for people with HFA and AS? We must ask ourselves whether the goal is to teach the children a series of rules and skills that we deem requisite for social interaction. Is it not more important to teach people with HFA and AS to value themselves for who they are? They must, of course, learn not to be totally egocentric and keep the perspectives of others in mind. But this does not require them to be something that they are not, only to be truly who they can be. As we join them on the journey, we can all learn to value and celebrate difference.

References

Attwood, T. (1998) *Asperger's Syndrome: A Guide for Parents and Professionals.* London: Jessica Kingsley Publishers

Attwood, T. (2000) "Strategies for Improving the Social Integration of Children with Autism." *Autism 4*, 1, 85–100.

Frith, U. (1989) *Autism.* London: Blackwell Publishers.

Frith, U. and Happé, F. (1994) "Autism; Beyond 'Theory of Mind'." *Cognition 50*, 115–132.

Gray, C. (1994) *Comic Strip Conversations.* Arlington, TX: Future Horizons.

Gray, C. (2000) *The New Social Story Book.* Arlington, TX: Future Horizons.

Sacks, O. (1995) *An Anthropologist on Mars.* New York : Vintage Books.

Sigman, M. and Capps, L. (1997) *Children with Autism: A Developmental Perspective.* Boston, MA: Havard Universtiy Press.

3

One Best Friend

Ruth Mandernach with Josh Mandernach

Writing about post-industrial society, Daniel Bell states in his book, *The Coming Of Post-Industrial Society* (1999, p.488), "The post-industrial society is essentially a game between persons. Now reality is primarily the social world – neither nature nor things, only people – experienced through the reciprocal consciousness of self and other."

What do we do with this statement? We, who have or work with children who have been diagnosed with any social-communication disorder, or have such a diagnosis ourselves. Do we throw up our hands in the air in defeat, admitting that the game cannot be played with any degree of finesse or confidence? To darken the room and allow our loved ones to interact solely with electronic devices such as the television set or the computer would be easy to do. To admit that the social interactions are so exhausting that they are not worth the effort would be another way out of this conflict.

Yet the essence of life can also be seen in people's reactions to our behaviors and accomplishments. The course of action I propose is to suggest ways of finding the one person who seeks out our child. The one person who desires to be in our children's space and home. I suggest ways of strengthening this connection by a strategic plan which requires an intensive amount of energy from the caregivers and significant others in our children's lives, but which can produce one best friend.

This is what I propose to achieve in this chapter: to write about the way to achieve not a pedestrian friendship (see Josh's Taxonomy of Friendship at the end of the chapter) but a best friendship. Having someone who always cares for them and calls them and wants to be with them on a week-by-week basis throughout the years can improve the child's self-esteem, increase their times of fun and joy and give them hours of practice playing the game of our post-industrial lives.

The reality of this experience is one that must carefully be thought through by the parent or caregiver. I have had the privilege of watching my son Joshua Mandernach and his friend Glen Darlington grow up together over the past five years. Their interactions have enhanced their quality of life. It is a journey for the whole family, one that impacts positively and negatively and results in a more empathetic sense of others and life. If individuals can have one positive social interaction then the odds of their seeking out another and another grow as they experience positive outcomes. This would be my hope for this chapter – that families undertake the commitment knowing what they are getting into and ready for the opportunity to help their child to discover new possibilites.

Choice of friend

> "I looked at him on the very first day of social skills group and knew we would be best friends."
>
> – Josh Mandernach (JM)

There are many ways to begin the process of building a friendship. Choosing the friend may take many forms. Teachers can recommend budding friendships to parents or group leaders can suggest children who have the same interests. By far the best approach is to have the child identify someone as a playmate. In Joshua and Glen's case, they say that they knew they would be best friends. The location of their meeting boded well for the relationship to continue. The set of parents were committed to seeking to strengthen socialization deficits by giving weekly energy, time and devotion to this needed area of maturation.

Families must be interested in this process as it may take a great deal of effort in gas, time, work and planning. The ability to share in the driving, alternate home visits and give the supervision needed is crucial. If only one side is interested, this long-term goal of having a best friend will not develop. So in addition to the children picking each other out, the families have to be amenable to the situation.

Parents often request and hope for their child's playmates to be out of the autism spectrum. They yearn for positive modeling, easy to watch children, typical behaviors and ease of presentation. In my experience I have found that can occur. Yet, our children take extra time and energy and understanding. Parents of children within the spectrum may already have that hard-earned ability. Glen's family, the Darlingtons, brought every needed quality and more to their friendship. They were eager for each child to have the time they needed together on a week-by-week, leading to year-by-year basis.

We were able to strategize ways to manage our children, gave the time needed to drive an hour each way, encouraged calls, had patience, grace and generosity that enriched our entire family.

Choosing the child entails choosing the family. Having another family around on a regular basis builds knowledge about disabilities and strengthens your own family while increasing your child's positive self-image.

Play dates

> "Mrs Mandernach, I believe you treat your guests better than you do your whole family and that just isn't right."
>
> Parenting tip from Glen Darlington

Planning this ongoing friendship has an effect on family life just like scheduling in a new activity such as music lessons or signing up for a team sport. Children within this diagnostic spectrum require some degree of regularity so that the joy of expectancy is not quashed. One meeting per week would be the ideal, with telephone calls or email exchanges in between. Again this is a commitment that requires time and follow-through. What a pleasure it is to have each child looking forward to their week time activity on a daily basis.

Play dates need be scheduled with the caregivers involved as well as the children. If the children are not consulted, they may well decline the opportunity simply because they do not enjoy surprises. This means that a phone call must include four people and that communication must be clearly stated and agreed to by all parties involved.

For the first four months keep the time short. One-and-a-half hours is plenty. This helps children to adjust to the new location and to interacting with a different family, and means few structured activities are needed. Also it gives the other parent a chance to get a handle on the new friend and his or her behaviors and needs. There is nothing wrong with them leaving wanting more time together. That in fact is a positive compliment to you and to the friend. They will look forward to the next week instead of wanting to call home to leave early.

Take the challenge of driving the children to new and varied locations to have a new sense of awe at the way their understanding of the world is translated. I have had many fascinating conversations with the young men. One December night while I was driving Glen back to his grandmother's home, we had the following conversation:

> "Mrs Mandernach, have you begun menopause yet?"
>
> "No I haven't Glen."
>
> "What age do women begin menopause?"
>
> "I guess I could begin sometime soon."
>
> "I was thinking that now would be a good time to start.
>
> "Why is that Glen?"

"Why because it is the coldest night I can remember."

"So you are thinking that hot flashes would help me be more comfortable now?"

"I was thinking that way."

"Well hold on to your seat cushions, I might just begin any second!"

Apparently Glen's mom had just purchased a book on this topic and left it in the bathroom where Glen had taken an interest and read it. This is a fun example regarding the interesting nature of autism, which can be full of surprises. The empathy shown here is heartwarming.

I have heard about my son's comprehension about family matters through Glen's restatements:

"Mrs Mandernach, I understand you went completely and utterly insane the other night."

"Well Glen I had a panic attack and was quite upset and scared."

"Josh told me that you were insane."

"I am 45 years old and have been insane for five hours. I think that is pretty good, don't you?"

"Well if you put it that way, I guess you are doing fine."

I would never have known what Josh was thinking if I had not heard this point of information from his friend. Take the time to drive; it will brighten your day to share in their insights.

Have the children plan a couple of activities that they would enjoy doing together. By setting up two centers on your own you are prepared in case they are needed. Perhaps a board game, art activities or an outside easy ball game would be appropriate. This is in case the quality of play declines quickly and they look at you with a blank expression of "What do we do now"? You will have prepared the siblings for the space needed in the house in advance. All will know what is going to happen and for how long.

Snacks are an opportunity for social interaction. Part of advance preparation is speaking with the family prior to the first play date to ask about dietary restrictions and most importantly food preferences. I was told to have white food for Glen, which is easy to accomplish. Milk, plain noodles, cereal and saltine crackers are examples of his favorite snacks.

One afternoon as I was washing the dishes, Glen was having a bowl of cereal. He proclaimed:

> "Mrs Mandernach, you are not looking at me."
>
> "No I am not Glen, I am doing the dishes."
>
> "You need to be looking at me."
>
> "What do I need to be seeing?"
>
> "I am pouring another bowl of cereal."
>
> "Yes you are."
>
> "I didn't ask you if I could."
>
> "In this house you may make yourself comfortable and don't need permission to have cereal."
>
> "Okay then."
>
> A moment later I began staring at him.
>
> "Mrs Mandernach what are you doing?"
>
> "I am looking at you. It's a joke Glen."

If the guests know that they are able to eat the food they want, they will relax and so will you. Quickly your child will be able to plan for snack time and be in charge of that event. He will be protective of his friend and make sure he is happy and full.

Play dates are fun only when planning has taken place and everything is in ready. The joy expressed by the children will show appreciation and love.

Level and type of play

> "I tried something new today, Mom. When I wanted to
> get his attention, I wrote: 'Time to listen to what I have to
> say.' That seemed to do the trick when I placed it in front
> of his face."
>
> – JM

Socially, children in the autism spectrum are years delayed. This
impacts greatly on their ability, interest and choice of friends.
Enter the arena where typically developing children versus
children within the spectrum vary the most. Parents who are
proponents of their offspring spending time with undiagnosed
children have a chasm to jump in this area.

Examples which describe their socially delayed characteristics
are easy to come by. Our children, who are in their teens, still love
to dress up in costumes, run around and engage in make believe
activities. They need some guidance regarding what activities to
engage in or else they may say, "We don't know what to do now."
Drawing is still a wonderful pastime as are computer and video
games. Since they will not have the opportunity to play some of
these activities with typically developing children, encourage
these important developmental levels when they are together.

Bluntness and forthrightness are hallmarks of their interactions. Do not be concerned that they will tell you from time to
time: "I'm bored," "I am not comfortable at this exact moment," or
"It is time for me to leave." This frankness helps you know what to
do to alleviate their distress and return fun back to their time
together.

Supervision is required to reduce the amount of time they are
in isolation from one another. Each tends to withdraw and is
thoroughly content with this setup. Within each play date some
time alone is understandable. It is tiring to be with other people
and in a different home. Stamina in this area needs to be built up
gradually. Yet for the supervising caretaker, it is almost distressing
to see this aspect of their diagnosis so clearly displayed. The same

can be said for the siblings who see the friends sitting in chairs in different rooms reading. The question will arise, "Why do they even bother to be together if they are apart?" Another situation is where one is playing computer games while the other is building a Lego space station, neither one thinking about the other. Enter the supervisor! Let them be alone for one third of the time they are together. Then remind them that they are in the same location so that they can interact and have a great time together.

For the time of together-play, prior action is needed. Josh and Glen have found that talking over the telephone or on email is a part of the day. They then plan what they want to do together and the visitor can bring the necessary equipment, books, journals, games or pads of paper. This way they are on the play offensive. Having plans helps to eliminate indecision, increase anticipation and helps the supervisor know what space is needed and what their other needs will be. Practice on the telephone is helpful to their everyday social skills. It is also a great release for them when they cannot get together. They have been known to spend one hour on the telephone but the usual length of time is ten minutes. Privacy seems to be important during these conversations.

Preparation is the key to successful events. The friends are the instigators and the family knows what will be happening. Communication has occurred prior to the time and supervision is warranted. Increased self-esteem and happiness are two of the outcomes. It is worth the effort and enjoyable to provide this opportunity.

Family implications

> "I am really nice to my friend's parents. I eat what they serve me, say thank you for having me over and am polite to them. I know that if I want to be with my friends I have to be nice to the parents. If the parents don't like you, you will not be in their house."
>
> – JM

The entire family is part of the friendship process. It is fine to define the disability that they are viewing. Hopefully, this will increase empathy, understanding and patience. My other children usually do not have friends over when Josh has his friends here. That seems to be a plan on their part, as children with special needs seem to need room. They can be loud, move in on other members' space and cannot read the social nuances which enable smoothness and peace to reign.

When the visits begin, there may be behaviors to understand and try to cope with, which takes energy. It can be tiring to ease children into social respect and encourage fun when that is one of their missing pieces. Keeping the length of time down is also a balm for the family, as they know when the ending of the visit will arrive.

Having closed doors does not seem to mean anything to the friends at first. Part of the rule-setting is to ensure that the family members have their own space. Discussing rules can be wearing, as the logical assumptions one family has may be completely different from those of another family. Hence the supervisor is in a position of having to use kindness and firmness to explain things in order to smooth the visit. Being consistent is crucial so that all are in sync and aware of the process.

After each visit, there needs to be a check-in time with the family members. This action may not take a long time, but it needs to occur every time. The family can share their own strategies about future visits and new rules needed. They can ask about strange behaviors evidenced and maybe express frustration or pleasure at the progress in the friendship.

In actuality it is helpful to have more heads involved so that you do not have to go through it blind. Many times the visit will go well, but occasionally there will be questions to ask the parent of the visitor. Families who have children in the autism spectrum are fairly used to this and usually not too defensive. This questioning and strategizing will go on indefinitely so that each will be used to working on the goal of a continued friendship.

Meals can be a particularly interesting time. Remember the bluntness spoken of earlier and paste that on to the dinner hour. While the supervisor may be used to these types of declarative statements, the family members may find it off-putting. Dietary narrowness may also be of concern to the siblings who cannot understand why the number of foods liked is limited and who may respond negatively to the opinions of the guest. Explaining that the purpose of a friendship is not to increase the gastronomical experience (which may happen), but to accept the friend for exactly who he or she is, sets the boundaries for the siblings and helps ease the meal time experience.

Recently, Glen was over at our home for two meals. For lunch I decided to take the boys out to a fast food restaurant. I asked Glen if he liked Carl's Jr. He told me no. I asked him if he liked Burger King. He told me no. I asked him which fast food restaurant he enjoyed and he told me, McDonalds. I said that we would go there. He looked at me and stated, "You do not love your children very much. They do not like McDonalds the best. It makes no sense that you cater to my desire when you should love them more and do what pleases them." My son Nick explained, "She is doing that because you are the guest and we want you to be happy and honored." Glen replied, "That makes no sense. You should love your own children more than me." I have not been able to convince him on this social protocol point of view. He believes that I am not a fine parent since I give him more say-so on certain issues.

The next meal was dinner. Glen came into the kitchen and asked what was for dinner. He mainly eats white foods so I had prepared turkey, mashed potatoes and corn. He proceeded to call his mother and I took him home before dinner. I knew he ate turkey but what his mom told me later was that he only eats turkey on Thanksgiving.

The family will end up feeling proud of the friendship over time as positive changes occur as a result of its success. As one invests time and energy, the outcome can be measured by the growing importance each friend has for the other. We care about what we put our hearts and minds into, and the rewards are in clear view as the ability to interact and the appreciation of each person in the family is highlighted.

In the future

As the children grow up more opportunities will present themselves. They will be able to play for longer periods of time. This will include meals with the other family, which is an important socialization opportunity. Overnighters are possible as are summer camps, birthday parties and day trips. Josh and Glen have made presentations to conferences and support groups regarding their friendship.

Josh has had many friends in his life but his friendship with Glen is the most significant. They have not outgrown each other and remain developmentally similar. Staying within the same diagnostic group has encouraged this steadfastness and understanding. They can describe each other's strengths and weaknesses in their usual frank and blunt manner. I can recall very few times when they hurt each other's feelings. This is due to the fact that they understand each other and can empathize about the difficulty they have within the social environment.

Josh has developed a taxonomy of friendship to help him understand the social nuances of friends. I hope you enjoy it and can refer to it as needed.

Joshua Mandernach's Taxonomy of Friendship

Best Friend	A best friend is a best friend. This is obvious and need not be defined.
Next to Best Friend	Someone who is a good friend but not your best friend.
Friend	You are on okay terms with this person.

Sub-Friend	A sub-friend is someone with whom you hang around occasionally.
Hang-on Friend	A hang-on friend is a fall-back friend.
Long-Distance Friend	You would spend more time with them if it were not for the distance factor.
Associate Friend	This is like the friends that adults have in their jobs. You know them but not in a close sense.
Pedestrian Friend	With this friend all you do is ask them stuff. When you see them around you say, "Hi!".
Annoyance	Someone you like but is aggravating to you.
Enemy	Someone you do not like who does not like you.
Archenemy	A person with whom you are in constant competition.

4

My Second Smile

Jim Nye with Calvin Nye

"Why do people say 'Sleeps like a baby'? Babies don't sleep that well." I listened, and felt that feeling that few people know; I felt my second smile.

The quote was an observation by Cathy O., who was my son, Calvin's, preschool teacher. We were having a conversation about teachers who have or don't have children, and about how you don't really understand what having children is all about until you have children of your own. Cathy O. is now raising her own two young children and the realization that children don't sleep that well through the night had really amused her. I agreed – children really don't "sleep like a baby." I was able to smile a second smile, because terms like "sleeps like a baby" now have a different meaning for me too, as my eleven-year-old son Calvin is diagnosed with autism spectrum disorder. Cathy O. had an exceptional influence on my son and our family.

> Yes, I remember Teacher Cathy. Everything I know I learned from her
>
> – Calvin.

As an infant Calvin was up past eleven o'clock at night cuddling with us, which wasn't so bad. It was the just-before-four-in-the-morning pouncing-on-my-belly looking-for-someone-to-play-with that almost did me in. How did he get out of his crib? Why didn't he tire of this game? Somehow, I found the strength in my belly, and the desire in my heart, to get up and play with the strange little man I named Calvin. I am so glad I took the time to understand him.

> I really liked playing with you, too, Dad. I liked the bouncing. I didn't like it when you threw me off
>
> — Calvin remembers early morning horsy back rides with Dad.

As new parents for the second time, my wife Cathi and I were much more relaxed with Calvin as an infant. I didn't wonder how you taught a child everything they need to know. I understood from observing Cassandra, our first born, that children can make sense of things and can learn on their own. I wasn't particularly worried about our baby boy's future. Calvin had been an easy delivery, and was healthy and alert. He was different from our then fifteen-month-old daughter Cassi just by the fact that he was born a boy. We expected a boy to be different. As time quickly passed, Calvin developed into a typical child with a bright future. He was a gorgeous baby, big and healthy, with beautiful brown eyes. He could be a little independent, a little overly focused and a little tuned-out. He was like his dad, or his namesake – the lead character in the comic strip *Calvin and Hobbes*, by Bill Watterson. He was just as charming, too. We were too busy being proud to notice any problems that we might need to be concerned about. Small things like eyes that darted around a lot and would come to rest on corners and floors. Like how he didn't like to go into strange rooms. Like that he loved being cuddled by his parents, but would stiffen in the arms of strangers. Even after we noticed some developmental delays when compared with our daughter, our pediatrician reassured us with the standard "Give him some time, boys develop slower than girls." In fact, long before we had even a clue that Calvin had any issues with his environment, we used to kid around that he was *selectively autistic.*

I was afraid of the floors. They were moving around like they were hot. I didn't know if I was going to be vaporized, or burn up like toast, or be attacked by a monster with really sharp teeth

> – Calvin recalling how he was terrified
> of the cafeteria floor.

We stopped kidding around when visiting my wife's sister, Leslie, who is a speech pathologist. She said that our handsome and bright boy was not just delayed in his development, but showed signs of having serious communication problems. Calvin was two years and three months old at the time Leslie tested him. Her results indicated that Calvin had the communication ability of a fourteen-month-old child. Being good parents, we went to our doctor, our school and our insurance company. We took him to speech therapists, had his hearing tested, fitted him with hearing aids. We tested his cognitive, physical and emotional development and his environment for the causes of his communication problem. Our house is not painted with lead based paint. We tested all kinds of theories, ideas, fads, philosophies and diets. A professor told my wife that she was "corporate mom," (yes, the Refrigerator Syndrome diagnosis from the 1950s), that we were controlling, uninformed and in need of counseling to accept our son's limitations for a full and happy life.

Calvin's language had not developed much beyond five words; the most frequently heard were "Mom" and the approximately 20 ways he developed to say "no." We used to watch him in a long closet door mirror practicing saying "no" with different intonations, using different faces and different expressions. He was very expressive and had a Disney-like range. His primary emotional teacher at the time was the movie *Fantasia*, and he had memorized every nuance and movement. I wasn't too concerned about delays in his ability; everything would come in time. He was only 21 months behind, and of course he was smart enough to catch up. Then I heard that he might not develop the language areas in his brain if he didn't show signs of progress soon. My resulting panic was directly related to my not being able to accept that prognosis, and I decided that my son was going to learn how to talk.

Calvin loved horsy back rides. I mean really loved them, obsessively. Getting a horsy back ride from Dad was one of his pure joys in his life, and our horsy back rides were my major pleasure contact with my son. It was how we got up together, and how we went to bed together. I imagine that he took 30 plus rides on my back daily, and my daughter usually had her turn if she was around, too. The rides started before he turned one, and by now he was almost three years old. I used to think that they were a great way to stay in shape. Now I was thinking that horsy back rides were going to become my reward for Calvin's learning how to talk. At the time, all I could get out of Calvin was "Hoshee."

I was in his face all the time, repeating "Daddy, would you be a horsy, please?" I would get "hoshee" three times in a row, then he would get mad at me. I know he hated it. He would growl and screech like a dinosaur when I wouldn't supply him with endless horsy rides. His guttural sounds and screeches were just the start. Hitting and kicking soon followed, but I would not give in. I was told that I was being mean. I was told that I was not respecting his autism, and that I was going to damage him somehow. Soon I was able to get "a hoshee," then "be a hoshee." Then came "Daddy be a horshee," and the ever important "please." As the son of a scoutmaster, manners were of the utmost importance to me, and I still believe that you can get away with a lot of deficiencies in life if you are polite and have manners. With "please" I relaxed a little, and there was a lot more give and take. Everything was still very rote, but I started to work on tone, and soon I was able to get Calvin to focus and say "Daddy be a horsy peas." I remember when Calvin faced me, looking up and off to the left, and said "Daddy, would you be a horshee pease?" I shrieked and hollered and scared him half-to-death as I hugged him hard. I was crying, and I am sure he was wondering when he was going to get his horsy back ride. He continued to get horsy back rides until he was eight years old, and he always asked for them in polite full sentences.

"Daddy, would you be a horsy, please?" easily led to "Daddy, would you get a milk, please?" and to his credit, my son is one of the most polite boys anyone could meet, and he is always one of his teachers' favorite students.

> It sounded like a monster when I walked, or a lion when I roared. It echoed so bad I couldn't understand anything. Before I learned how to talk, you sounded like the ocean. I didn't like them at all. They felt funny in my ears. Remember when I threw them out of the car window, or took out and hid the batteries?
>
> – Calvin remembers wearing hearing aids.

When Calvin was four he used to take off his hearing aids, hand them to me, and say "Shut up." I was just so happy that he was beginning to initiate conversation. I had since stopped worrying about what other people thought, or the thoughtless comments that passed for advice. It was then that I began to develop my second smile.

"Shut up" was Calvin's way of letting us know that he didn't need hearing aids, something that I suspected. But when we were staring at brain stem auditory test results, was it hard to argue with the findings that he was partially deaf. Calvin was enrolled in a preschool hearing impaired program, with four students who were totally deaf, and four who were hard of hearing. I could tell he didn't belong there when I dropped him off on the first day. He just didn't interact with the other students like the other children did. But it was not a total waste. He learned to look, he learned to sign 'bathroom', 'thank you' and his name. He also started to pick up a vocabulary. After five weeks, one of his teachers called us in for a consultation. She showed us a chart with six catagories of Calvin's areas of weakness. Some of these we knew about, some of these we suspected, but all together it was fairly overwhelming. As a mother of a special needs child herself, she said our best course was to go right to the experts, and directed us to UCLA's Neuropsychiatric Hospital. After several tests, the two interns took a torturous 30 minutes to tell us our son had "high functioning autism." What a relief! We finally had an answer. Or so we thought. We asked what we should do next. Gosh, you would have thought that no one ever asked that question before. We were handed a card for a support group that met on the campus. This is when we met Linda Andron, became part of the UCLA Family Support Community Program and joined the other families on a different journey.

> I heard about "painting the town red" on the TV, probably a cartoon. Since we didn't live in a town but in a house, I thought I would paint the house red
>
> > – Calvin gives a reason why he used red to "paint the town red."

My daughter Cassandra ran upstairs very excited, and screamed that Calvin had painted the kitchen red. I ran downstairs as fast as I could, but it is a big old ranch house. I found Calvin had painted one spot on the cabinets. With a proper amount of scolding, I cleaned the spot off with paint thinner. I was quite relieved that it was not worse than one spot of florescent red paint, left lying about after Halloween decorating. When I walked outside, I almost died. Every hub cap, reflector, vent and light of our car, truck and Airstream trailer were sprayed with a generous shot of florescent red paint. All over the details of the house, flowers in the garden, doorknobs, windows, bikes and toys, fresh red paint was dripping.

I grabbed the gallon of paint thinner and raced around dampening everything red, and gave Calvin a five-gallon bucket full of soapy water and a big brush. He could barely move the bucket and was protesting, "Too big!" and "I can't." I was too furious to care and he did move that bucket and work hard under duress for the first time that I could recall. He told me that he was sorry several times. Then he said "Gee Dad, you are really doing a good job." I was amazed that he created such a long sentence by himself. I was still furious though. After an hour of my yelling and our cleaning, Calvin began to sing "Whistle while you work, do-de-do-do-do-de-do..." I broke down and cried. My second smile was very big in the twilight of that evening. If you look closely, you can still see red paint in the crevices of the Airstream.

Calvin entered Cathy O.'s class as a very curious boy. He was bright and inventive and basically well behaved. We still had to throw him into the arms of another person because of his fear of floors. Cathy O. took to Calvin very intensely. She found that if she sang questions to him, he would respond by singing back. For months he wrote "f.h.e." on everything. One day, while watching television with Calvin, I saw the "f.h.e.," Family Home Entertainment. His vocabulary grew rapidly at this time. Then one day, while Cathy O. was on the phone and delayed in attending to Calvin, he went up to her desk, tore up a piece of paper, stapled it together with another piece of paper, and created a large Tyrannosaurus Rex with a moveable jaw. Out of nowhere came this big work of art that still hangs in our living room. It was the first of many amazing pieces of art that Calvin has created. At the bottom of the paper background are the big "f.h.e." letters that he signed everything with. He doesn't use those anymore. He also gave up his Barney tie, black coat and top hat that he used to wear every day.

> "My sister's and my secret language is a secret, Dad. I feel too embarrassed to tell anyone about us."
>
> – Calvin protesting about my desire to tell his secret.

> "Okay, how about if I buy you that new Nintendo 64 game you want so badly?"
>
> – Dad, smiling.

> "Well, that's a deal."
>
> – Calvin, smiling too.

Calvin has relied on Cassi to help him out his whole life, and in ways I imagine will never change. We relied on Cassi, too. She is a very sweet, understanding and helpful girl. Cassi was also the only one who could understand Calvin during his first three years.

I imagine that a lot of their language development was due to being related, being the same height, having the same needs, and being in proximity to each other. I also know that Cassi could just understand Calvin in ways that are not easily explained. They communicated through a series of facial gestures and mumbling that attempted words. I am sure that Cassi quite often relied on guess work, but there was a clear ability to communicate too. Waves of the hands coupled with eyebrow gestures had meaning. Biting the lower lip while raising eyebrows meant he was hungry. That furrowed brow meant he had to go to the bathroom. Even I knew that one. I didn't know the difference between Calvin's request for an apple and banana, but Cassi did. They both have trouble explaining it, and are not able to communicate like they once did, but there is no doubt in my mind that they did communicate. If you really want to communicate with someone autistic, you need to go to his or her level and imitate them.

> Well, you were Stimpy because you were the bigger one of the two of us
>
> – Calvin explaining why he was
> Ren and I was Stimpy.

At one time Calvin had the typical autistic's need for no one, unless he wanted a drink or to watch some TV. He didn't interact with my wife Cathi or myself much beyond getting his basic needs met and getting cuddles or horsy back rides, and his back scratches, a desire he inherited from his mother. One day we were watching cartoons and this really strange one came on called *Ren and Stimpy*. All of a sudden Calvin was quite animated, and was mimicking the every movement of this strange and deranged little Chihuahua named Ren. Much to my surprise, I found myself in the part of the big slow cat named Stimpy. It was thrilling to be involved in a part of my son's life that he was creating, and if we needed this TV show to help us in doing that, great! I also found myself getting punched and jumped on a lot.

I was amused to find Calvin reenacting the very same scenes playing on television. I can remember when he would run into a dinner party, babbling incoherently at everyone, and I would see an episode in his actions. I'd warn everyone that in this "scene" Ren would kick the shins of those next to him, so be careful. Everyone would just look at me puzzled as I escorted "Ren" out of the room, sheepishly smiling my second smile.

Now Calvin is now fully included in a fifth grade general education classroom, and is doing better that I ever imagined possible. His teacher Jan B. has had Calvin for a year now, his first teacher without an aide of any kind, and they are doing a fantastic job together. I am a big supporter of full inclusion. Because of inclusion, Calvin has a large circle of friends. His friends invite him for overnights, attend his birthday parties, and call him for advice on the latest video games. He still has his pet tiger "Hobbes", his Ren and Stimpy dolls, and is forever embarrassed for having affections for a particular Barney tie.

Calvin still accuses me of making him "not autistic," especially when he is frustrated with being normal. He has his own "second smile" and has thanked me for helping him become who he is today. The fight was worth it.

5

How to Speak Asperger's

Fran Goldfarb with Guthrie Devine

One day, when my son was five, I went to pick him up at his after-school program. He was sitting on the bench, again. When I asked him why he had been benched, he said, "I don't know, I didn't do anything wrong." Now this was not the first time I had heard him say this, and I knew, in all likelihood, he didn't have any idea of what he had done wrong. I asked his teacher for an explanation, and she informed me that he had been fooling around on the swings and she told him that if he didn't stop, he would have to leave the area. Well he didn't stop, and so she told him to leave the area. Fortunately, I am fairly fluent in Asperger's and so I was able to figure out where this communication fell apart. She meant the swing area, but he thought she meant the school, so he left. Once again, a teacher thought my son was extraordinary in his ability to misbehave. Once again, my son thought that he was being punished unfairly and once again, a disciplinary action was unsuccessful because it taught him nothing.

Learning to speak Asperger's is as important a skill for parents and teachers as learning social rules is for children with Asperger Syndrome. Very often our messages are confusing and do little to help our children learn how to operate in our (foreign) culture. We are so familiar with our slang, idioms and sayings, that we seldom notice that they convey little useful information. I once said to my son, "The ice you're skating on is very thin" (meaning you're skating on thin ice) and he responded, "Well the ice you're skating on is very cold." Whose statement made less sense? Another time I came home from work complaining about how "pooped" I was. This comment occurred during our extended and fairly tense period of toilet training, so you can imagine the look of horror on his face.

Communication is very complex. It depends on understanding the words, the tone of voice, the expression on the speaker's face, the context of the remark, and often relies on the listener's knowledge of the speaker. It is often said that dogs don't understand language, they respond only to the tone of voice. Well people with AS often only pay attention to the actual words spoken, without integrating the other clues. Because of this, they often miss irony, humor or important emotional cues. Their interpretation is literal. I have also found, because so many things in their lives don't make sense, they often don't ask for clarification because this is just one more thing that doesn't make sense. When I asked my son if he really thought that the teacher would tell him to leave the school, he seemed surprised by the question.

Another problem with communication can stem from thinking in very black and white terms and from the inability to accept exceptions to rules. To my son, a rule is a rule is a rule (unless he is stressed at the time and can't remember it). I was once summoned to the same after-school program with the directive to pick up my son and *bring bleach*. Words that strike fear in any mother's heart. My son had urinated in the sandbox. The teachers were beside themselves, they had given him ample opportunity to go to the bathroom but he refused and then went and urinated in the sandbox. Again, my goal was to clarify what happened, not find out who was wrong. My son kept telling me that he couldn't go to the bathroom because there was no one to go with. The rule at this program was that a child had to go to the bathroom with a buddy. This event occurred late in the afternoon and there was no other boy to walk with him to the bathroom. One of the aides offered to go with him, but he understood the rule to be that you went with a child, not an adult. He was in a terrible double bind: does he break the rule by going with an adult or does he try to hold it in? He held it in as long as he could. No one thought to explain to him that if there is no buddy available, he could go with an adult. Again, he was punished for following the rules.

Additionally, if something is true once, then for the child with AS it is true forever. My son develops rituals and traditions after only one encounter. He came with me one day, when I took one of our cats to the vet. We had been there a long time and my son was very thirsty. He (very politely) asked if he could have a drink and was told that he could help himself to water in the staff lounge. Several months later, when he came to the vet with me again (we have three cats), he immediately went into the staff lounge and helped himself to some water. The receptionist was, of course, taken aback – imagine the nerve of this child to think he could have the run of the place. It was hard for my son to understand that if permission is granted once, it doesn't mean that you don't have to ask permission the next time. The rules in our culture for what is appropriate are so confusing; sometimes children are expected to know what is okay and are ridiculed or scolded if they ask and sometimes they are expected to ask if something is okay before they do it. While parents feel that it is important for their children to ask if they don't understand something, we must help our children accept that their questions will not always be welcomed.

Add to rigidity in language the very strong desire to do what they want to do and you often have a recipe for your children looking for loopholes. Getting morning jobs done is often a struggle in our house. And, like most other parents, we have tried almost every strategy there is. A common technique is using a desired activity as an incentive, such as, "You can look at that magazine after you have gotten dressed." Of course, I interpret that remark to mean after you have done all of your morning jobs and, of course, my son interprets it to mean after he has put on his clothes (but not brushed his teeth, combed his hair or put on his shoes). You would think that I would have figured out the problem by now and sometimes I am careful to say that he may look at the magazine after he has completed his morning jobs. But there is something bigger going on here. I want him to do what I want and he wants to do what he wants. Since we have had this encounter so many times, my son should know that getting dressed equals all the steps, not just putting on his clothes. So, is this just a simple misunderstanding, or is this manipulation? Just because a child has Asperger Syndrome, it doesn't mean that he isn't going to do what other kids do – try to manipulate their parents. That is why it is important to have an understanding of what is typical behavior for a child of that age. Also, because children with conditions along the autism spectrum are developmentally delayed, they may be operating in a way that is appropriate for a younger child. Consequently, it is important to sort out when your child needs clarification and when they just need consequences.

The inability to integrate non-verbal cues is often a problem for people with AS. They can easily misinterpret a situation because they fail to notice shifts in intensity. When I ask my son to listen to my voice to see if he can tell whether I am calm, impatient or angry, he is often unable to make that distinction. He has learned when I ask that question I am seldom happy, so he usually guesses angry, but the tone of my voice doesn't give him clues that I am running out of patience. Most children can tell when their parents mean business and when they need to start paying attention. If the tone of my voice or the expression on my face isn't meaningful to my son, how is he to know when it's time to get with the program?

Likewise, we often use facial expression, body language and the context of the situation to help interpret or reinforce what the speaker is saying. If you are unable to integrate all of those clues, you often miss the point of the conversation. These clues also help you to know the other person's reaction to you. Are they bored or anxious about something, are they trying to end the conversation because they have to leave? Learning to speak Asperger's involves more than understanding each other's words; it often means helping our children understand the social etiquette that surrounds our conversations.

Our language is littered with sarcasm and irony. The clues to when someone is being serious and when she is being sarcastic are often subtle and are easily missed by someone who takes language at face value. This can lead to misunderstandings or worse. Humor may also be difficult to understand, again because it is so often based on irony. In the same vein, we are often baffled by the things my son finds hilarious. My son has a wonderful sense of humor. My husband and I love wordplay, so does my son – he enjoys making up puns and is clever and witty and spontaneous. But he also believes that if a joke was funny once, then it will be funny the hundredth time. This is another example of a developmental delay. You would expect a three- or four-year-old to retell the same joke over and over but a nine-year-old would know that the joke would soon wear thin. My son will often ask for clarification about things we find funny. Many of his interests are quite mature, and so it is easy to forget that he often doesn't understand some of the subtleties of humor.

Social communication is one of the most difficult areas for many children with AS, because communication is so much more than just exchanging words. It involves an understanding of the prevailing culture, manners and norms. It also involves being accepted as part of the community. So much of what we do is intuitive and doesn't always seem logical. Social distancing is an example of this. Different cultures have different ideas on the appropriate distance to be from someone else and this can change depending on the situation and the level of intimacy you have with that person. We have all had the experience of talking to someone and they were standing too close. We experience a certain amount of discomfort. Now imagine if you had no sense of what an appropriate distance was, but it always seemed to be different than what was comfortable to you. My son is often standing too close to people and sometimes touches their faces or leans on them. Family will try to explain why this makes people feel uncomfortable, other people who don't have the same investment in my son will simply think he's weird or avoid him altogether.

My son is willing to go into stores and ask for help. But he often has difficulty accomplishing this with grace. He finds it hard to figure out when it is his turn to talk and will try to ask his question when a salesperson is busy or is helping someone else. He often forgets to say "excuse me" or "please" and consequently he is often viewed as rude. He recently wanted to buy something at an amusement park gift shop. Although the salesperson was waiting on someone else, he kept trying to give her the money. She politely told him that she would get to him soon, but he was unable to notice that soon meant when she was done with her current customer. He was also unaware (that when he finally paid) he should get change and started to leave without it. The look on the salesperson's face (as he was leaving) told me that he was not the style of customer she was used to. But he can also be quite charming and because his requests are frequently more mature than you would expect from a nine-year-old (such as "Where are your Champagne Grapes?") he frequently gets much more help than you would expect. Children with AS often appear gauche and need lots of practice to do even simple things like buying something.

Children with AS often have trouble with the social rules in a classroom or in other group situations. If he is interested in what is going on, my son has trouble recognizing that he isn't the only one the teacher is speaking to and treats a lesson like a conversation – shouting out answers and not letting other children have a turn to speak. And since he usually knows the correct answer or has an interesting tangent to go off on, he can easily take over a discussion. Conversely, if he isn't interested, he can be very disruptive. It is one of his major life goals to have interesting things to pay attention to and he will do whatever he has to do to make things interesting if he is bored. This trait has been problematic in other situations such as tours. He is fascinated by so much, and wants to learn so much more, he often tends to monopolize the tour guide at the expense of others.

Managing the playground can also be difficult. Children with AS can often play with one friend, but when you add additional children things get much more complex. It is often difficult for them to compromise to get a consensus on what or how to play. Other children perceive their enthusiastic suggestions as being autocratic and may tend to shy away. A child often needs help to understand other children's behavior and to manage their own frustration and anger. Other children also have to learn how to listen to the ideas of the child with AS, because often they are terrific.

One of the most frustrating aspects of AS is how inconsistent kids can be. Sometimes my son just doesn't "get it" and sometimes people come up to us in restaurants and tell us they wish they had our child. There are times that my son is the easiest child in the world and times that he seems to be the most difficult. Tony Attwood talks about "A" days and "B" days, with "B" days being those days when everything is just harder. My son loves this concept because it helps him to explain that there are days when he is more sensitive to things and more difficult to reach. He doesn't always know the reason, but he knows there are days when even if he tries his hardest, he can't manage as much as he can on "A" days. Just as we find him harder to manage on some days, he finds it harder to manage himself. One day he was playing with one of our cats, or rather he was trying to get the cat to press the button on an electronic noisemaker. He kept saying, "Push the button, Gus" and of course Gus ignored him. This went on for about ten minutes and finally Gus got bored and left. Well, my son was following him around the house repeating, "Push the button." My husband and I were laughing both because we thought it was only fair that our son get a "taste" of what it's like to get his attention and because I realized that all cats have AS. When I shared this observation with my son, he said, "I don't think that's right, because when cats don't listen, it's *always* because they don't want to." Out of the mouths of six-year-olds.

My son loves rules and he is very concerned with having good manners and interacting with other people. He loves conversations, he loves listening to other ideas and sharing his own. He knows he should say "please" and "excuse me," he knows he shouldn't interrupt and he knows he should say "hello" and "goodbye." Why then do some of these rules fly out of his head just when he needs them the most? The world is a foreign place to so many children with AS, often they think they are doing the correct thing and it backfires on them. This can make many situations stressful. I know that when my son is worried about a situation, it is hard for him to pay attention to anything other than his anxiety. This makes it hard for him to remember the rules he cherishes so much. He is also very shy in new situations because they are also very stressful. He may act very goofy at first, hiding behind me or running away, but if he is allowed to get used to new things, he warms up and becomes quite charming. He often tells us that he is very uncomfortable until he gets used to something and then he can't figure out why he was so resistant. It is our job to remind him of this when he is feeling shy.

Although it seems that my son often misses non-verbal cues, I find that there are situations such as talking on the telephone when he really needs them. He really doesn't have any connections to the telephone; I used to think that he was the only child in the world who had never answered the phone – not true, but pretty close. He also dislikes making calls but will talk on the phone. But he says talking on the phone is confusing, language that he can understand in person turns mysterious when he's on the phone. He finds that this is a situation where language becomes more literal for him. As he says, all telephone language confuses him.

Sometimes communication with my son seems to be delayed. He can be so obtuse sometimes, but if I can wait until he has pulled it together, he can be so insightful. One day, I took my son for some blood work. This is something that we do frequently and usually we go before school. This day seemed like any other, until I heard from his teacher. He had arrived at school about an hour late and proceeded to have an awful day. Everything was a problem, he was disruptive, he refused to do his work, he walked out of the class and more. When I asked him what the problem had been, he told me, "I don't know." About three days later, he came to me and told me out of the blue that it is too disruptive for him to arrive late at school. He doesn't know how to get started if things have started without him. He asked if we could go for blood work at a different time. Now we go on Saturdays. It took him three days to put his experience together, but when he did, he did it beautifully and with a built-in solution.

My son hates surprises, good or bad. Because he intuits so little, he likes to have things to be as predictable as possible. Part of learning to speak Asperger's is learning about the advance work that has to be done. After another rotten day at school, which involved a lot of time in the "time out" room, my son was able to tell me the problem – he had been at therapy and when he returned, his desk had been moved. His teacher was doing a little rearranging of the classroom and had moved his desk about two feet (not what most people would consider a big deal, if they noticed it at all). This was during a time when we were re-modeling our kitchen and our home was chaotic. There wasn't a surface to put things on and we couldn't cook. I asked him if he got so upset at school because it reminded him of home. He said that home didn't bother him because he had been told in advance that this was going to happen, but school had been a complete surprise. Although the disruption at home was far greater, the early warning was all that he needed.

So how do we learn to speak Asperger's? We pay attention. We see which situations confuse and frustrate our children. If we learn to listen to our language through their ears and view our culture through their eyes, we will see the inconsistencies which are confusing to the uninitiated. But just as I am learning to tell my son that he can read his magazine after he finishes his morning jobs, it isn't enough just to watch what I say. I must use my knowledge of Asperger's to serve as his guide to help him to understand the intricacies of our language and social culture. In a way, I am his translator and so I must also tell him that often people will say "get dressed" and mean doing all the things to get ready to go to school.

There are several strategies that can help you prepare your child to understand the world and the world to understand him.

Humor

I use gentle humor for a couple of reasons: the world is serious enough and it is easier to learn when you are interested and enjoying yourself. It is important that the humor must be about the situation, and not at your child's expense. The humor must be used to lighten the load, not as a way to ridicule. We use word plays, puns, rhyming and any other way we can play with language. The more you play with it, the less literal it needs to be.

Explain, explain explain

So often, the advice we are given tells us not to use too much language with children who have language-processing difficulties. However, I find that the better my son understands a situation, the more likely he is to comply. He was playing with his cousin at my sister's house one day. When I came to pick him up, I reminded him to thank his aunt. He wouldn't, even after several prods. Finally I asked him why he wouldn't say thank you and he replied, "I don't know what I'm thanking her for." Once I explained why he should thank her, he was happy to do it.

I find I am often deconstructing events and conversations with him. It helps him to understand even if the best explanation is "It doesn't really make sense, but this is what people do." A wonderful book that he loves is "On My Own" which explains the feelings surrounding many situations and strategies for handling them. Just having this information written down helps.

Check your child's interpretation

To help him communicate, it is important to understand his perception. Just like his leaving the school instead of the swing area. I can't help my son if I don't understand his view. Telling my son to do something is often a three step process: 1) Asking if he heard me (often he has lost me at this point), 2) Asking him what I said (he may have heard me, but he may not have processed the information) and 3) Asking him what he is going to do (just because he has processed the information, it doesn't mean that he has understood my intent). Taking him through these steps is so much more useful than just getting impatient because he "wasn't listening" again. It is equally important to check his interpretation of something he is trying to tell you. You may be off base, which can be frustrating to him when he is trying to get his point across.

Tell him your process

My son loves to hear stories about how I learned things when I was a child or young adult. It helps to reassure him that everyone can have trouble with communication sometimes. Once when I had just learned to drive, I was going to something at UCLA. I was driving around the circular drive when I saw a sign that said "Do Not Pass." So, I pulled over to the curb, and couldn't figure out why other cars went past the sign if I couldn't. My son loves that story. It provides a commonality, as he can understand my bewilderment.

Notice and anticipate

Pay attention to what is difficult for your child. Our job is not just to react to our children's difficulties but to anticipate what might be a challenge. In this way we can help prevent some of life's dramas. If I know that a change in environment is difficult for my child, I will help him to prepare for it and allow him to come up with strategies which are helpful. In this way, we not only avoid a meltdown, but he learns that he has skills and ideas that are helpful.

Practice and rehearsal

It is so important to prepare your child whenever possible. When my son is getting ready to do something stressful or new, I like to go over the rules with him again. When he needs to talk on the phone, we often rehearse the conversation. Carol Gray's *Social Stories* and *Comic Book Conversations* are great ways to help your child prepare for new or difficult situations. The more practice he gets, the more likely he will be able to draw on that resource. We often put together lists of several strategies and then he can use the one that feels best.

Educating others

Lastly, I don't think it is solely his responsibility to adapt to our culture. I believe it is important for our culture to become more tolerant of people who are "different." Any encounter that he mis-understands needs to be explained not only to him but to the other party as well. I am often telling people how their message might have been misunderstood and how they could convey their information more clearly. Additionally, his teachers and the other grown-ups in his life have to learn to resist the temptation to attach a motive to his behavior. Not understanding is different than not willing to cooperate. It is easier on everyone's nerves and more likely to result in a favorable outcome if grown-ups can view this as a failure to communicate and not just a failure to comply. It is important for people to understand how hard my son works most of the time just to be where he is. If they are willing to meet him at least partway, what a terrific experience for both of them.

Understanding Asperger's is like learning a new language and a new culture. But this is the culture of your child and he must learn not only how to fit in, but how to be comfortable in his own skin.

Introduction to Magic Show

Guthrie wrote this book when he was seven. He wasn't writing about Asperger Syndrome, but it turned out to be a beautiful allegory. It tells the story of an alien who is charmed by a magic show. He never understands what it is all about, but he is able to enjoy it and embrace it and make it a part of his own culture. This is how it is sometimes: our children may never understand all of what we are trying to communicate, but they may be willing to make it a part of their culture. To be able to enjoy without always understanding, that to me is magic.

 Magic Show

by Guthrie Devine

Once there was an alien invasion. On board the ship there was an alien named Fff. Fff was interested in discoveries, not destroying where he could find them.

 Fff decided to spy on the building nearby. So he went.

The sign said "Mothage", the Fff put on his special reading glasses for earth language and it said "Magic". He went inside. He saw a man in a hat holding a grey metal thing and leaning on a red box. The man called someone up.

He put the person in the box and used the grey metal thing to cut the box in half. And then he put it back together without glue. The person came out in one piece with no blood. Then the man said "If you think tricks that are easier to believe are magic… you're wrong. That was magic." Everybody clapped. Then Fff went to the gift shop and bought a magic trick book. He needed the page for the trick the man called "magic".

Here's the picture for the trick he saw.

Fff went outside, got in his escape ship and went to the ship in his escape ship. When he got there, he took out his pencil and drawing book. He drew lots of posters for magic. And then he went and made a hat like the one he saw the man wear. Then he got two boxes, painted them red, put a hole in the top of one and two in the top of the other. For decoration, he put glow-in-the-dark star stickers. Then he looked through his building books til he found a tool building book. It had a picture of the metal thing on it. He got to work on building the metal thing.

And then, it was time to go back to the planet… which was good, cause he was ready to do the magic thing. It took a long time to get back. But it was fine. When he got there, he put up his signs and he built a little place that said "Magic" on it. It had lots of seats, and a stage with two trap doors. The trap doors were for another trick he saw in the book.

Finally the building was ready. He got to work practicing the two tricks. Finally, the show was ready. He put a sign that said "TODAY" next to all the magic signs. People wondered what this magic thing was. Everybody ran to the building. Everybody gave an "ooh" and an "ahh" for each trick. Everybody went to the gift shop and bought magic tricks and trick books. It was better than Fff thought it would be. It was great.

References

Attwood, T. (1998) *Asperger's Syndrome: A Guide for Parents and Professionals.* London and Philadelphia: Jessica Kingsley Publishers

Navarra, T. (1993) *On My Own: Helping Kids Help Themselves.* New York: Barrons.

6

The Asperger Chronicles[1]

Jim Devine

Because these "Chronicles" started as a letter to a relative, a good way to get the ball rolling is with four (highly edited) paragraphs from that letter, which may evoke memories from other parents of kids with Asperger Syndrome:

> Thanks for your concern about G. I should clarify what is going on with him. I think it's a mistake for you to generalize too much from your very limited experience with G. We are "in the trenches" and we know there is something "wrong" or "special" about him. Telling us that our experience is wrong or wrongly interpreted (as your comments imply) is not comforting at all: it's telling us that what we see is irrelevant to the issues we have to deal with every day.
>
> People who don't deal with him daily or as teachers often see G as totally "normal", especially because he seems very bright and creative (at least to an objective observer such as myself!) and deals well with one or two adults. In fact, when he was in preschool my wife and I did not see very much of G's abnormal behavior, because we didn't see him very often with groups of kids with a

---

1   *Editor's note:* The story of the Goldfarb/Devine family continues with Jim's views of Guthrie and AS. Since this was also a journey of self-discovery of his own AS characteristics, he writes from a unique perspective.

117

teacher trying to structure activities, so we were also surprised by his troubles. But they are real.

He is not "autistic" in the normal meaning of the word: he's not the silent child who stares at the wall or dreams all the time (completely shutting himself off from society) or a younger version of Dustin Hoffman's character in the movie *Rainman*. You may have gotten the wrong impression from Mom's references to the readings I sent her on autism. They were really off-base unless interpreted very carefully.

The diagnosis has turned out to be quite valid, however. Once the psychologists pointed out that G had AS, all sorts of pieces of the puzzle started falling into place. Among other things, we discovered that a lot of his "bad" behavior was not intentional, but rather a result of his slow or incorrect processing of the information he gets from his social environment. That's what's meant when we say he is on the autism spectrum.

Before I got the letter to which I was replying here, G had been expelled from his second preschool, six weeks after his admission. The problem was that he couldn't cooperate or participate well in group activities such as "circle time." Further, he was extremely resistant to transitions from one activity to another and he was monopolizing most or all of the teacher's aide's attention. The actual expulsion happened because he reacted violently, hitting a kid with a block, when another kid interfered with a structure he had built with blocks – and broke his attention. I think he was pushed to violence by weeks of accumulating bad feelings, teasing from students, toilet accidents, and the like. Luckily, violent incidents have been very, very, rare. In general, G is not a violent guy and has felt quite bad after he has been violent.

Below are my thoughts about AS both as an observer and a participant.[2] The main parts relate to my son, "G", who was diagnosed as having AS by psychologists at UCLA in early 1995, when he was four. This was not very long after AS showed up in the DSM-IV, the psychologists' diagnostic "bible." I should stress that am not a psychologist; rather I am a professional economist who went outside my discipline to try to understand what was going on with my son, to help him. All psychological theorizing should be seen as amateur musing which is only intended to pose questions to think about.

A difference from classic autism, at least according to the official criteria, is that kids with AS develop language very early. Even at age four, G was using the subjunctive and the passive voice correctly, something many adults don't do or don't care about. However, that doesn't mean that he communicates well, on either the giving or the receiving end. There is much more to communication than grammar, as shown when other kids stare at him in amazement as he talks like a professor. Neither is it communicating when he tries to minimize the number of sounds he uses (for example when he said "mar?" to mean "May I please have a marshmallow?"). Too often, language is only a game for him, as when he uses Jar Jar's lingo from *Star Wars*.

G is very verbal, charming, creative, loving, and far from "mentally retarded," but he has a very abstract relationship with other people. That is, it seems that he connects to others based on his preconceived vision of how to do so, rather than following any kind of intuitive communication with them. He tends to be pedantic, to lecture people, both adults and other children. He's very good at quibbling and (alas!) could make a good lawyer.

He is very poor at playing with others of his own age – especially as the size of the group grows – unless he's telling others what to do. For his fifth birthday party, he thought up a game: pin

2   It overlaps with the old version which is online at Barb Kirby's invaluable OASIS page (*http://www.udel.edu/bkirby/asperger/*).

the head on the dinosaur. He gave instructions to his grandfather about how to make the equipment and to the kids about how to play it, rules which the adults didn't quite understand. I think the kids did, though. Maybe he'll be successful in Hollywood, since he loves to direct!

One time he was at a fast-food restaurant, playing in the play structure. He insisted on telling a kid one or two years younger than himself all about *Star Wars*, his obsession at that moment, rather than telling his brother, who was closer to G's age. I also think the younger kid didn't know English well, while the older one did! This event was repeated, two years or so later. He played with another kid that he hadn't met before: the kid was two to three years younger, while the topic was again *Star Wars*. Luckily G has other obsessions. But I think that *Star Wars* should be declared the official movie of AS. Or should AS be declared the official syndrome of *Star Wars*?

Another time, he lost a toy at the park. He went all over the play-structure announcing over and over again, almost like a butler at a door, "Has anybody seen my plastic cellular phone that plays music? It's a toy." I don't think he connected with any of the kids enough for them to even think of answering.

He also does pretty well when he's in the mood to follow other kids or a teacher's directions passively. This can be a problem, since in his social naivete he sometimes imitates kids who are severely emotionally disturbed, who stand out in a crowd as doing interesting things. (We try to keep him out of that kind of situation.) But it's all or nothing: either he leads or he follows – he doesn't participate well as a peer except in very small groups.

Unlike some autistic people, he lacks "splinter skills": he can't do anything like correctly multiplying large numbers in his head or composing new and beautiful music from memory without knowing what it sounds like. But the results of his psychological testing look like saw teeth: lows (in arithmetic, for example) are combined with highs (in more abstract math). Similarly, though he scores low on social skills and emotional intelligence, he has flashes of brilliance that still amaze me. He's extremely good with pattern recognition, and is able to put shapes together into coherent patterns very quickly.

G also does not have Attention Deficit Disorder, though some of what he's "got" is similar in some ways: sometimes (often!) it is very hard to get his attention. Early on, my wife was afraid that G was deaf and tried clapping her hands behind his back. Instead of being deaf, he hears too much – and has a hard time deciding what's most important, what to pay attention to. But G seems to be able to focus tightly on a single topic for a long time (if it's something *he's* chosen to be interested in), and he gets very irritated when his attention is broken. In trying to deal with all of the stimuli he's bombarded with, he tends to over-react, to build a wall that's *too* impervious to stimuli. He is very good at concentrating on something that he's interested in, but finds that he has a hard time paying attention to anything else or making a transition to some new matter (such as going to the bathroom). This helps explain his expulsion from the preschool discussed above.

By the way, I think it's much more pleasant to think that G doesn't listen because he has a hard time filtering out stimuli, rather than because he simply doesn't *want* to listen. It's also better that his toilet-training problem and similar issues have been more than simple defiance.

His "attentional problems" are symptom of his (mild) form of autism: one of the problems with AS kids is that they have a hard time understanding social stimuli because they are overwhelmed by all sorts of stimuli from their environments and from their own bodies. It's a little like always being distracted by aches that move around one's body in an unpredictable way. This fits with some of his strange but apparently harmless activities, such as hitting himself ("self-stimulation"), because he's trying to prioritize stimuli. He's also over-sensitive to the fabric of his clothes. We have to cut off the labels in the necks of his shirts, while my wife is frustrated by his aversion to blue jeans. Lately, he's become very sensitive to the phone ringing and to car alarms going off.

One of the issues that came up at school is his propensity to run away from the teacher and the class, often toward the street. He once ran away four times while on a field trip near downtown (not a safe area). His running away seems to be partly based on his poor social connections. Not feeling at ease with a group, he runs away to see something that's interesting. I think that he knows that he shouldn't run away, but his poor impulse control gets the better of him. This can also be seen when he pushes buttons and touches things that he shouldn't, setting off burglar or car alarms.

G's lack of physical coordination is also common among those with AS. I think his lack of physical coordination may be related to his filtering out of external stimuli. Maybe he is so clumsy because he gets too many signals from, and thus filters out too many signals from, his own body.

But he doesn't fit all of the criteria for AS. Unlike most, he has a wide variety of interests (or obsessions) which tend to change from week to week or even hour to hour. But his failure to fit exactly into the box of the psychological definition is no problem. Probably the majority of those seen as fitting in this (or any) psychological category do not fit all of the criteria, since people are too complicated and too varied. Such categories should be used to help us understand what's going on (or to get support from schools, insurers, etc.) rather than to create stereotypes that limit our thoughts.

It's quite common to use these categories too much, as with the common academic debate (which often pops up at our parents' support group) about whether or not there's a difference between High-Functioning Autism and Asperger Syndrome. All of these psychological categories are like points on a map – one with many dimensions! Some real individuals are close to the points on the map but others are not, instead they are between them. Thus, even professionals can have a hard time deciding what category to put someone in. There is no objective test like there is for diabetes or some other physical illness.

AS is one point on a "road" on that map called "the autism spectrum," so it's called a "spectrum disorder." G is somewhere near that point. The road reaches from hard-core, classic autism, to Asperger Syndrome, to more "normal" behavior. Complicating matters, an individual may also have additional conditions (say, obsessive-compulsive disorder).

G needs special attention and that is what he gets. Because we hired a professional advocate and went through an appeal process, the school system is helping to pay for it.

G also gets play therapy, which is the use of play (with an adult) to exhibit emotional themes and events in G's life. It's a substitute for the "talking cure" that most adults get when they go into psychotherapy. (We let G keep his play therapy time secret. It belongs to him.) G's play therapy started with two main goals:

- To deal with his difficulty in separating fantasy from reality. For example, G was *extremely* serious about being a vampire (and about being adopted from the fictional island of Bibidina) for what seemed to be a year. The psychiatrist figured out that these fantasies were not really serious (as with schizophrenics) but instead it was a *big* game. Interestingly, simply visiting the psychiatrist and talking about Bibidina somehow convinced G to abandon these fantasies. But he still has very strong, obsessive, attachments to some of his fantasies.

- To deal with his depression. He tends to have chronic depression, which luckily is not very deep. This is often associated with AS, probably due to the fact that people with AS don't deal with social situations very well but really want to connect with people.

In addition to all of the academic and psychotherapeutic stuff, we also signed him up for karate lessons, swimming lessons, gymnastics and, most recently, soccer. We're hoping that he will learn some self-discipline and physical coordination from these sports. AS is a "developmental disability," which means that it isn't an absolute barrier as much as one that takes a long time and hard work to conquer.

My own experience

Dealing with the fact that my son has been labeled as having AS has led me to the realization that I'm "Aspergerish" myself. I used to think it was just an inferiority complex, lack of self-esteem, that kind of thing, but the more I read and think, the more I think I'm also "high-functioning Asperger's" (after almost 50 years of learning to deal with it). Otherwise, I can't understand why I have really weak emotional connections with my family and friends, why I fail to mourn at funerals, why I spent a lot of my youth drawing maps of imaginary places, watching old movies on TV that I can't remember, and so forth.

Even before I had heard about AS, I read an article about Donna Williams (one of the most famous people with autism). My immediate reaction was that it sounded so familiar. Just like her, I sometimes find myself getting over-stimulated, unable to deal with all of the things going on. (I zone out in department stores and other places where there are too many stimuli.) Her story helped me understand how the TV can totally *grab* my attention away from people and other stimuli.

Once I realized that these problems existed, I got better at preventing them. My feeling is that G will learn how to do this too, though he's likely to have a lot of trouble during junior high and puberty.

I do think that low self-esteem has something to do with my problems: AS makes me feel inferior or depressed, which makes it harder to climb over the barriers created by AS.

Not being a mental health professional, I really shouldn't diagnose myself. Even professionals shouldn't do so: medical students often think they have each disease they study. But the AS materials seem to fit my experience. It is a useful working hypothesis, to be modified as I gain greater self-understanding. I hope that it doesn't bias my reporting in a way that simply throws back what the theory says instead of giving people authentic insights into the problem.

I think I'm over a related problem, that of seeing AS everywhere. I've speculated that a whole list of well-known people, from Albert Einstein to Bill Gates, fit the AS mold. But since there's been no "official" diagnosis for those people, it's all idle speculation, a parlor game. Furthermore, diagnosis does not help those who are deceased or who are not interested.

To move away from that kind of thing, it is useful to restate and examine the definition of AS from an article by Christopher Gillberg in Uta Frith's book *Autism and Asperger Syndrome* (1991). These six main criteria are completely interrelated, but I'll try to separate them.[3]

Severe impairment in reciprocal social interaction

I have a hard time interacting with peers except on a superficial emotional level; sometimes I can do better on the intellectual level. I can't say that I have any close friends except my wife (and I would guess I'm not as close to her as most husbands are). I don't have a group of people I hang around with when I'm not working. I usually feel uncomfortable with groups, alone in crowds. I either get too excited or "zone out" from the group altogether.

When school is in session, I'm lucky that there is a standard lunch crowd that I can join. I like the group, but often find myself frustrated that people don't react to what I say. It's probably a matter of my not understanding that they *are* reacting, because non-verbal cues are too subtle for me to understand. I know I sometimes speak too loudly in an effort to get some attention. I probably repeat myself too much, for the same reason. When I'm not clearly the center of attention, sometimes the best I can do is to interject one-liners.

---

3   They represent an alternative to those of the DSM-IV.

I recently realized that I was telling variants of the same joke to a colleague over and over again. I also was doing so with another, but he does exactly the same thing. There are a lot of professors with AS-type symptoms. Academia attracts people with AS the way business attracts sociopaths.

As for "socially and emotionally inappropriate behavior," I can think of all sorts of different cases where I did things that just didn't fit in, as well as the unnecessary repetition. For example, I've often been sitting at a table in a cafeteria and inappropriately intervened in a conversation at a neighboring table. (I do the same while waiting in line, an activity I hate with a passion.) I was having a hard time filtering out that conversation, was stimulated by it, and jumped in, completely out of place. There are many worse examples than that which haunt me now and then.

I have recently found that email can be the kind of social situation I can deal with well. I probably participate in email discussion groups too much. There are three reasons I feel right in this kind of "social situation." First, I am usually bubbling over with ideas: I read someone's contribution and often find myself stimulated to think about it and then come up with some idea or some connection with some other field or discussion. Luckily, the social atmosphere of the groups is very informal. (I've learned never to state my views as *conclusions*, but as questions or as working hypotheses.)

Second, as you've probably noticed, I tend to think in paragraphs rather than sentences, with all sorts of thoughts that only make sense when put into context with each other in an orderly way. I can do this over email. Third, *everyone* on email has a hard time picking up social cues; people have to be trained to communicate without getting into all sorts of silly disagreements. For example, people have to use little "smileys" (such as :-)) explicitly to indicate that what they say is a joke. Due to the nature of the medium, I am far from alone in my Aspergerish behavior.

Some people complain that the email "community" isn't real, pointing out that it lacks face-to-face communication, it's hard for more than two people to participate at once, etc. But at least it helps people like me feel better. This point is similar to one made by Linda Andron, the director of G's social-communication group: she argues that we shouldn't insist that kids with AS have "normal" friends. Instead, we should realize that having a friend with AS is just as good, if not better, since the point of having friends is not to live up to some social standard but to contribute to one's happiness.

All-absorbing narrow interest

I don't fit this one very well. Like G, I am not the type who's totally obsessed with a single interest, excluding other activities and emphasizing rote more than meaning. I have a bunch of different interests (though maybe the scope is too narrow) and I'm extremely interested in the question "why?", rather than mere description. I'm pretty abstract, while a lot of folks with AS think very concretely.

My wife says I repeat myself a lot, as have others. I've tried to reform myself on this and I think I've largely succeeded. I have three thoughts on this though. I think everyone, including my wife, repeats a lot. It's just easier to notice others' repetition than one's own. Second, some of my repetitiveness is simply due to a poor sense of how to make "small talk." By the way, I do not bore people with long-winded discussions of my work and hobbies, since I don't think they are interested. Instead, I just don't talk about them. Third, most of my repetitiveness is in my mind and is not vocalized, perhaps because I lack the self-esteem to blab on and on when I think people aren't interested.

Imposition of routines and interests, on myself and on others

I don't think I impose routines on others very much, if at all. Instead, I guess, my response is to try to avoid situations where I feel it's necessary to impose my routines on others. I am much better at avoiding routinization of my own life and interests than I used to be. I do have my routines, such as excessive playing with the computer and too many visits to the email program to see if I've received any new messages. In the morning, I like to get up long before anyone else so that I can have a quiet time to get ready for the day (while drinking too much coffee). I get very irritated when anyone else gets up too early and breaks my routine.

I don't know if this has any connection with AS or not, but sometimes I have a very weak sense of what it is that I like at all. Especially when I was young, I got interests or ideas of what is good from others. About 20 years ago, I realized that I didn't have my own laugh, that I was imitating other people. This might make sense in an AS framework because it is an extreme. Whereas those with AS typically have very self-contained visions of the world and are very determined to stick their views, I tended to go all the way to the opposite end, to absorb others' views in an effort to fit in. I don't think I do that any more, since I no longer take on and imitate others' viewpoints, because I've developed a clear and logical system of thinking about the world for myself.

Speech and language problems

I don't know if I had delayed speech development speech or not, or whether I had perfect grammar or peculiar voice characteristics when I was young. I doubt that I have them now. I do know that I take pains to avoid overly formal and pedantic language. This is partly a reaction to being too formal and pedantic in the past and partly a rejection of the pretensions of academics.

I have a hard time with social cues and therefore sometimes find it difficult to comprehend things that people say. I often have a hard time with idioms and sometimes I take words too literally. For example, if I say, "I hurt my thumb," my wife says "I'm sorry." I used to respond, "It's not your fault." It is only recently that I stopped taking this phrase literally.

Furthermore, it was only relatively recently that I realized that I was assuming that everyone else used irony all the time and that this assumption was wrong. It was also relatively recently that I realized that I had to avoid being ironic all the time, since most people didn't get it. It's more common for people with AS to miss irony altogether, taking everything literally, but my case is a kind of polar opposite that fits with the AS tendency to go to extremes.

In social situations, I tend to have a script prewritten in my head. It does vary over time (since I make an effort not to be boring), and I sometimes am very spontaneous. I make an effort to write my scripts to allow for spontaneity that isn't socially inappropriate.

I have a hard time with being interrupted, especially as my wife and son do it all the time. Recently I heard "Miss Manners" on the radio: she said that not all interruptions are impolite; some interruption involves participating in someone else's conversation. I guess a lot of my wife's interruptions are of this sort. I have to learn how to distinguish the two types of interruptions.

As for pedantry, there's no doubt that I like to lecture. I'm probably an excellent lecturer (in my humble opinion) but I am not a good teacher in terms of the ideal of a small liberal arts college. I'm not very good at interacting with the students and I have to make a conscious effort to relate the economic theories I present to current events or to the students' own concerns. A lot of the time, however, I just don't put in the effort.

This laziness about teaching may arise from my tendency toward perfectionism (something that G shares). Often, I decide that perfection can't be reached so I simply give up. I also tend to be interested in absolutely everything, so that drags my attention away from teaching. I guess one can connect these things to AS.

Non-verbal communication problems

One thing I've always found diffcult is knowing whether or not someone likes me. It's this kind of thing – not realizing that one is liked by others – that is depressing and encourages people with AS to be depressed.

I probably move my gaze about much more than other people do, not looking at their eyes (though I'm better at this than I used to be). I'm always seeing lots of different things that can easily distract me from a conversation I'm having with someone. One way to avoid being distracted I've found is to have one single object to concentrate on besides the person I'm talking to. A while back, when someone was visiting us, I found that I had an easier time hearing what she was saying – and keeping my attention on her – if I toyed with G's Lego. It was something trivial that distracted me from paying attention to all of the different things that could distract me from her, even though it was impolite. I've been thinking of getting worry beads – they are better than smoking, after all.

Motor clumsiness

I definitely suffer from this! I am highly embarrassed to admit that two or three times I've hit my wife and hurt her – totally through my clumsiness. Luckily she didn't get a black eye or anything and didn't take it personally (as far as I can tell). Of course, another reason I've always had problems with athletics is that I "space out." I remember being the center in touch football games (a role that the other kids thought involved the least athletic ability) and missing that it was time to hike the ball. In graduate school, I played soccer a few times, exhibiting the other extreme. I would focus entirely on getting to the ball and kicking it, almost entirely ignoring the other people on the field. (Some experts say that autistics treat other people like pieces of furniture.) I would kick the ball in the right direction, but not as a pass to someone else on my team.

Now let me tell you how more specifically how it feels. As my wife says, it's as if I am always speaking and hearing a foreign language and I always have to translate from that language to my own and back again. This feeling pervades my whole life, even though I deal with it much better with it than I used to. Temple Grandin, a famous person with autism, describes her experience as being as if she's an anthropologist from Mars. That fits my experience; following this, this chapter is titled the "Asperger Chronicles" to mimic Ray Bradbury's *Martian Chronicles*.

Years before I had heard of AS, I told two academic friends that I felt like an "alien in human society." They said they felt the same way. (In hindsight, they seem Aspergerish too, though I know only one of them very well.) A lot of the institutions and ways of life that most people treat as "normal" seem to me to be arbitrary and strange.

In summary, I may or may not fit the criteria for AS. But at least looking at Gillberg's list has helped me with self-clarification. If I have an Asperger-type "personality style", it is not a very bad case. Since I wrote my original "Chronicles" I've met adults with AS whose problems are far more serious than mine. Tony Attwood's excellent book shows a diagram showing the autism spectrum, reaching from classic autism to High-Functioning Autism, to AS, to "loners." I'm in the last category.

References

Attwood, T. (1998) *Asperger's Syndrome: A Guide for Parents and Professionals.* London and Philadelphia: Jessica Kingsley Publishers

Frith, U. (ed) (1991) *Autism and Asperger Syndrome.* Cambridge and New York: Cambridge University Press.

7

Making Friends With Aliens
Inclusion and Collaborative Autobiography

Max Lisser and Jennifer Westbay

"I wanted to prove that sign wrong," said Max of his second-grade teacher's back-to-school "Welcome" poster. "Mrs [X]
does *not* love children!" Despite mediation, the school site's
cordial and talented special education coordinator, numerous
planning meetings, and a good deal of home-school communication, Max could not withstand the assaults of full inclusion in
second grade. For two months, September and October 1997, he
suffered a rigid daily schedule and an assaultive environment that
were modified very little to meet his needs. The teacher, nearing
retirement, showed no apparent wish to engage in further professional development; she was hardly the "life-long learner" called
for by the Consortium on Inclusive School Practices, and in fact
did not attend the district's in-service training about Asperger
Syndrome. (If you were traveling into alien country, wouldn't
refusing a road map be more than a little arrogant of you?) At the
same time, the aide's considerable knowledge of classic autism
had little to do with Max's way of being. Both teacher and aide
seemed to think of Max as a typical kid acting naughty, not an AS
kid doing his best. To them, Max was peculiar, not creative; incor-
rigible, not cordial. Basically, we've all come to think, both
teacher and aide could not surrender control – of the students or
of their reputations among their colleagues – a major block to

successful inclusion, according to Marsha Forest and Jack Pearpoint (1995). The teacher probably does love tractable, color-within-the-lines children, but Max was right: she did not love him. Her students, at first full of good will, quickly modeled on the grown-ups in the classroom, and, Max said, thought him a "weirdo."

Max's parents (Max's dad and I) must take some responsibility for this reaction. At age five, Max had entered the same school's inclusive multi-age classroom for kindergarteners and first- and second-graders, but Mom and Dad had not formally introduced him to his new friends. Although they had offered to visit his peers before his arrival, the building principal and the district's special ed coordinators said, emphatically, "No thanks." Mom and Dad acknowledged that friends, not strangers, usually introduce strangers. Besides, Mom and Dad were ambivalent about the ethical issues. Max didn't know about his diagnosis at the time ("But I've always known I'm different," he says now), so why should his peers? Should his first identification to new classmates be as a kid-gloves kid?

Over time, this situation calcified into a kind of conviction: an ethic of privacy and the application of policy meant that, in Max's case, full inclusion came to mean full silence. Even after Mom and Dad had told Max about his AS, they kept it private from others, sharing the diagnosis only with need-to-know professionals and some fellow parents. In the inclusive classroom where Max had begun elementary school, this nonsensical sink-or-swim strategy had been more or less successful, if success is measured by academic achievement, manageable behavioral idiosyncrasies, and not too many tantrums. But if success means the opportunity for Max to be known and loved for who he is, he deserved more respect and support. When he would later write, "My new friends, I want you to know me," he could mean it fully. But in second grade, this had been a bad equation: lack of candor with peers, plus willfully benighted traditional classroom teachers, equaled disaster. After two months, Max was taken from the inclusion setting, and from November to March, he lived in limbo, spending schooldays first in an alternative setting, and then at home.

After one last confrontation between Max and his teacher, he was given an interim alternative placement, the school's resource room for fourth- and fifth-grade learning-disabled students. The topic of the confrontation, ironically, was writing. Since Max had learned to talk, he had composed remarkable stories with engaging characters and a discernible beginning, middle and end. He loved to invent adventure plots that, often, his pre-school teachers wrote for him to illustrate; at home, he dictated for his parents to input and print out. Kings' birthday parties, Cuban drummers, pumpkins that talk – like most other imaginative kids, Max was learning his own voice through his fiction. But in Mrs X's second grade, Max resisted daily morning journal-writing. He was simply not interested in assigned topics, and when he could choose his own, he interpreted the fifteen-minute writings as more significant than daily practice for fluency. So even though he had generated some topics ahead of time, he took a long time to select one that was important to him – and then to get going with the writing itself. One morning, however, Max had made a good start on a subject he did care about, and he continued to write after the other kids had run out to recess. When the teacher told him that she wanted to lock the room and take her own break, he resisted, and eventually he threw his pencil at her.

In the long view, the resulting punishment may have been a blessing. After a 45-day alternative placement had ended, Max had a bout of the flu. Mom had taken a leave from her job and after Max's recovery continued to work with Max at home; he read and wrote as much as he liked, visited museums and the zoo, completed practical math activities around the house and at the market, completed science experiments on the kitchen counter, and went to karate or the library or the movies in the afternoons.

At last, following mediation and negotiation, Max was to enter a new school.

Inclusion and the presentation of self

We – Max, Mom and Dad – were hopeful but leaving nothing to chance this time. It became clear that we should use the family forté to ease the transition to the new school. All of us write. Max has his stories. Dad, a screenwriter by training, now owns a company that writes marketing materials for business clients. Mom teaches in a writer's program at the university; her syllabi focus on the rhetoric of popularization, or how writers transmit esoteric knowledge to nonspecialist audiences. The school continued to insist that parents not prepare and present oral introductions between Max and his new peers (though parents of diabetes patients are in every classroom every year). Instead, we all agreed, writers write. Story-telling, marketing, popularization – here were our talents, all characteristic of well made self-descriptions. We were all sure that if his new schoolfriends, both kids and grown-ups, knew the authentic Max, he would have a genuine chance of succeeding at school.

Though Max was and is the principal stakeholder in this transition, the autobiography we wrote was not exclusively a self-portrait. It was a family project – hence the "collaborative" of the chapter title. After all, very little of most writing in the real world belongs to a single author – the business proposal sounds like a single voice, but is a product of many hands; below the reporter's by-line is a news story that owes much to editors; heads of state revise speechwriters' words before addressing the nation. In our case, Mom facilitated Max's composition of his life story. The intended narrative was not composed independently; neither was it merely a chronicle of a life. Given the family's contentions with the school district, the self-description was as much persuasive rhetoric as narrative (as is most communication, declares the title of a recent book by dicourse specialists Andrea Lunsford and John Ruszkiewicz, *Everything's an Argument*). Events and insights from Max's history would not only introduce Max to his new classmates, but argue his right to be in the classroom and help readers to reach the same conclusion. In fact, then, the process of writing the booklet had begun long before the difficulties of second grade, in Max's story-telling, and in his parents' study of the power of writing to make social connections between communities.

Our inspirations

Our writing had several mentors, both local and more remote, both visual and written. A parent from Max's preschool, also an education advocate at our local Regional Center, told Mom how she had introduced her own son, who has Down's Syndrome. Using the concepts of same and different, she asked kindergartners, "Who likes pizza? What kind of pizza do you like?" The children learned that although everybody enjoys pizza, people prefer various kinds. Then, for an audience of five-year-olds, the comparison of pizza to people was made explicit.

While the advocate had told us about a parent presentation, a videotape had shown us one. UCLA's Family Support Community Program, which Mom and Max attended weekly, had produced a videotape series, "Thank You for Trusting Me." In one segment, a mother uses oral description, still pictures and video to describe her Fragile X son to the middle-school classmates that he is to join the next day. She too uses the same-and-different approach, beginning each section of her presentation with questions – about siblings, TV, sports and many other features of students' everyday lives.

Other parents have used writing to reach wider audiences for similar reasons. Mom's principal print influence was the Candian author Karen L. Simmons, parent and author of *Little Rainman: Autism – Through the Eyes of a Child* (1996), a family history focusing on a son with classic autism. It is a slim volume with oversized pages, and while it simulates a child's book, its length and the wealth of its popularized information targets older readers, who easily accustom themselves to the controlling fiction of the genre. Since Max's second-grade year, we've found similar advocacy for children on websites. For example, "Lezlie Cora Jensen", the description of a Minnesota kindergartner with a disability, is sub-titled "Pseudo-Autobiography by Liza M. Jensen"; one page of a site called "Joseph's Story" ends, "...He told me [the mom] that it was ok to write this because then maybe the kids will know that ADHD doesn't mean that he [is] crazy". The genre resembles the "as-told-to" celebrity autobiography. "Social stories" replicate this discourse for the subject-children themselves. Adult advocates – especially all parents – must often speak for children they love, whether they advocate *about* the child or narrate *as* the child.

But some of our most powerful influences were kids genuinely speaking for themselves. In an especially touching and instructive segment from "Thank You for Trusting Me," Alexis (see Appendix) explains her interests in film production and promotions, trusts her classmates with a self-description of her cri du chat, and asks for their understanding. Several other kids in same video package, all boys, describe the advantages and the challenges of AS. Although they excel in math and stand-up comedy, for example, and are given special passes at Disneyland and other theme parks, they know that their classroom behavior sometimes annoys other learners. Again, young web authors we've discovered since Max's school transition show remarkable ability to teach through written composition. The site *kidpub.org* published "Aspergers Syndrome: Finding the Path," an autobiographical short fiction by an English girl called Sara. "I based this story on my own experiences," says Sara, "to help other people understand my problem and the difficulties I and thousands of other kids face every day." Our family wanted Max's new schoolfriends to learn from his autobiography the self-knowledge we've observed in Max himself and in these kid-narrators. Max had much to show his audience: both *information* about the effects of AS on thinking, on imagination, and on behavior, and the *tone* of self-awareness.

The composing process

As a result of these influences and thoughtful planning, Max's book shows him to be serene, coherent, in control. The actual composing process, then, could be a little messier and yet result happily. Brainstorming was the first genuinely collaborative activity as Max and Mom began to generate content for the book. We thought about what Max was good at – an astonishing array of skills – and what he enjoys most. There was so much to say, in fact, that we had to select carefully, perhaps a knowledgeable writer's hardest job when addressing a naïve audience. (Still, like Simmons' *Little Rainman*, Max's autobiographical booklet is long, so long only loved ones can find it continually compelling.) Sitting together on the sofa, Max and Mom chatted, Mom taking notes in second-grade-style printing that Max could read and edit. Or sometimes Max paced and talked, paced and talked, and Mom recorded his extemporaneous thoughts the way both she and Dad had done for years, as a word-processed document. Mom added her own details, items that seemed to her to be both true to Max and potentially interesting to a second-grade audience. Our mission at this stage was to use concrete detail and assertive style to characterize Max as a normal, capable kid with interests and skills – the kind of boy classmates and teachers wouldn't think twice about choosing for group-work and play-yard games.

Still, we had to guess what might be most appealing and instructive, for neither of us was addressing actual peers. Mom, who has no neurological diagnosis, isn't a kid, and Max, who is a kid, is anything but typical. And neither of us had met any of our readers. We were specialists addressing nonspecialists. As Einstein said of his mathematical theories, if I tell you the truth about what I do, you won't get it, but if I tell it so that you understand, I must lie a bit. We wanted to honor both truth and accuracy.

Max's parents' professional lives require hard thinking about audience, and they knew that the book would reach not only second-graders but also bystanders – ripple-effect readers. We could foresee Max's new special ed teacher, his new second-grade teacher, the district and school special ed personnel, his new classroom aide, the principal, parent volunteers in the classroom – but there might be other readers we hadn't predicted. In fact, we considered adults a key component of our target audience. Though Max was only in second grade, there was a certain amount of faculty-room and district lore already in process about him, and we wanted to anticipate and correct misinformation about the boy and his diagnosis. We *addressed* the autobiography to students, whose response was and is crucial to Max's success. But we *targeted* the educators too.

As details were described and chosen – details that Max wanted to share with his readers, details that would characterize Max usefully – we needed to organize them sensibly. Recalling the former second-grade teacher's failure to generalize helpfully from concrete details about Max's history, we evolved a "chapter book" structured topically and developed with explanations and examples. A chronological, suspense-driven story structure risked not engaging new friends sufficiently. Better, we thought, were short themes that expressed basic truths about Max and his AS. As a result, his autobiographical booklet embraces both narrative description and exposition, both showing and telling. Like our literary influences, and in accordance with our inclusion goals, chapter headings emphasize Max's "specialness" – both struggle and triumph.

Although the autobiography focuses understandably on its first-person narrator, as an introduction, it reaches out to the reader. A number of references to popular culture, especially kid-culture, connect Max to his peers. Even those allusions and illustrations that accompany descriptions of Max's eccentricities emphasize that he's a regular kid who owns pets, participates in some sports, and watches Saturday morning TV. Rather than sit back in passive bemusement, the child reader is invited to engage in specific writing, art, and speech tasks; some ask for simple recall while others require more active critical thinking and application of concepts – but nothing so demanding that it takes attention from engagement with Max himself.

Because one of Max's talents is a remarkable drawing ability, and we have a houseful of snapshots, we could illustrate the book liberally with color illustrations. Although Max did not copyedit his story by hand (that was Dad's job), he paced the room, listening carefully enough to correct several mistakes and infelicities as drafts were read to him. (He also complained that Mom typed, scissored and taped far more than he thought necessary.) As a process and as a product, Max's story replicated our key inclusion goal – as the University of Alberta website on inclusive education describes it – to "let the child shine" in order to encourage "support from own-age peers." When our *magnum opus* was photocopied and comb-bound, it was ready for its audience.

Hi. I'm Max Lisser.

I am a second-grader new to Franklin School.

CHAPTERS

I want to get to know you, my new friends, and I want you to know me.

I like pizza, and probably you do, too. My favorite pizza is Numero Uno pan pizza with no tomatoes, extra cheese, and black olives. I'd be willing to bet that you don't like exactly that kind of pizza. Please write down your favorite kind of pizza here:

(That will help me learn a little about you.)

YOUR NAME	YOUR FAVORITE PIZZA
_____	_____
_____	_____
_____	_____
_____	_____
_____	_____

Most people like pizza, but they like different, special kinds. **I am like most people**, yet
I am different and special, too.
* * * * * *

MY SPECIAL BRAIN

One thing that makes me special is that I have not been part of a regular school classroom since Halloween. I have been schooled at home, or I have had my own personal teacher at school. So it may be hard for me to get used to being all day with other kids. I am looking forward to it, though, and I hope you will help me.

Another thing that makes me special is that I have **Asperger Syndrome**. (Listen to the sound of the word "Asperger"; I call it McDonkey's, just for fun. Get it? If you don't, look at the bottom of the page.) There aren't very many of us Asperger's people, fewer than one person in 500.

Asperger's is a **neurological syndrome** (say "new–ro–LODGE-ih-cul SIN-drome"). That's a fancy way of saying that your brain probably works differently from mine.

> **I do some things unusually well**. These are my Asperger's talents. At the same time, **I need unusual help doing other things**.

My special talents:

building sets	reading	art	computer games
telling a story	swimming		video games
remembering	music themes		board games
karate	acting	caring about my friends	

The "as" of "Asperger" sounds like "ass," another word for donkey. "Perger" sounds like "burger," which reminds me of McDonald's. So – McDonkey's Syndrome!

Because Asperger's people have big talents, some of them are really important. Here are examples of some famous people who probably had Asperger's when they were alive:

Albert Einstein was a physicist. He thought up the famous Theory of Relativity. For some people, "Einstein" is another word for genius.

Wolfgang Amadeus Mozart was a composer. He wrote more than 600 musical pieces, beginning at age five.

People tell me I am smart and creative and fun to be with. Maybe someday I will be famous too, and do good things to make other people's lives better.

Along with special **talents**, Asperger's people have special **needs**. Let me tell you more about the way my brain works.

- First, Asperger's people usually have interests that we can't help thinking about a lot and talking about a lot.
- The second thing is that most of my five senses are really powerful. Things that don't bother typical people bother me a lot.
- The third thing is that because of the way our brains work, we may have different ways than you do of controlling our tempers and showing our friends that we care.

Some of my own interests are so big to me that they might be called obsessions or manias. In **The Wind in the Willows**, J. Thaddeus Toad always had some mania going on, something he couldn't stop thinking about. For him, it was boats, then horses, then owning a car, then escape, then airplane flight, and so on and so on.

Me at the Petersen Museum acting like Toad in his motorcar

This book will tell you a lot about what I like. But when we are together, I need my space! The thing I hate most is being embarrassed, and I would rather you did not ask me questions. We can get to know each other by doing other things:

- We can play games together and work in classroom learning groups together.

- You could write me a note or draw me a picture about yourself. After all, these days I am meeting many new people, and you have only one new kid to meet – me.

WHAT I LIKE

Here's one thing I like: **ART**. I won first place for Grades K through 2 at my old school in last year's "Reflections" contest called "It Could Happen". Then I won third place for the entire Santa Monica–Malibu School District.

One of my drawings, a portrait of Harriet Tubman, was chosen to be made into a postcard to give to people who might contribute money to my teachers' art program.

I have some favorite places. I live on 18th Street, and I have lived there since I was 4 days old.

My favorite museums are the Petersen Automotive Museum and La Brea Tar Pits Museum. (Did you know that "La Brea" means "the tar" in Spanish? So when people say "the La Brea Tar Pits," they are really saying "the the tar tar" pits!) I had my sixth birthday party at the Gene Autry Western Heritage Museum and my seventh birthday party at the Museum of Flying.

My favorite hotel is Excalibur in Las Vegas.

My favorite theme parks are Disneyland and Sea World. I like zoos too, and I have been to quite a few of them. My favorite stores are Super Crown on Wilshire and F. A. O. Schwarz in New York City. One of my favorite houses to visit is my grandmother's in Minnesota because she has deer and geese and a lake right outside her windows. I got my Darth Vader outfit at an F.A. O. Schwarz in Minnesota.

My favorite place of all is New York City. Last summer I lost a tooth at the top of the Empire State Building.

I bet you like museums, lakes, and fun stores, too. My favorite restaurants are I Cugini and Polly's Pies. I liked Dive! in Century City, too, and I'm sorry it closed.

What are your favorites? ✏️ 📋

_____

_____

_____

I have told you what I like. Here is something I don't like – being embarrassed. One time at my old school, I came into the classroom from the computer room. In front of all the kids, the teacher said, "Welcome back, Max." I didn't like that.

Here is something else I don't like – getting teased. Another teacher said that she didn't think other kids were teasing. I think that it doesn't matter if she thought it was teasing or not – what those kids were doing hurt my feelings anyway.

Here is one more thing I don't handle well – losing. Sometimes I am a good loser, but if I really care about a game or contest, I get very angry if I lose.

- I must be **taught** some things that probably come naturally to you – things such as making and keeping friends, and controlling my temper.

I sometimes lose control when I am embarrassed or hurt or frustrated or angry. I might hit or kick someone, or start shouting. I use the word "hate", or the word "kill"; sometimes I say "shut up". These words don't mean I do hate – just that I am very, very upset.

One time my friend kept whispering dinosaur sounds in my ear. I told him to stop, but he didn't. The teachers couldn't tell he was annoying me. I asked for their help, but they didn't help me, and after a while, I hurt my friend. It was a very sad moment.

Sometimes I get upset with people when they don't understand me. Can you and I make an agreement?

- Please ask me nicely if you want me to do something or not to do something.
- I will try to ask you nicely if I want you to do something or not do something

HOW I MAKE MYSELF MORE COMFORTABLE SO THAT I CAN KEEP CONTROL (OR GET BACK CONTROL)

I have learned that some things make me feel better. I will tell you about them so you'll know when I am trying to control myself.

If I am uncomfortable with what people talk about or ask me to do.

I change the subject.

When I can't think of how to join in a conversation,

I may say something from a book or a movie.

At Douglas Park one day, I told a kid, "Unhand that!" a line from Robin Hood. And sometimes I call my pals Monique and Guthrie "Skraaldians," aliens from the

Saturday morning TV M.I.B. (Men in Black). If you don't know the story I'm quoting, you may be confused.

Sometimes when I can't think of what to say,

I may not answer at all.

(By the way, I like to swim for many reasons. One of them is that it is quiet under water, and I am in control of my movements. But I also really like to play with friends in the pool or at the beach.)

Here's another thing that makes me feel good:

balancing and bouncing.

I like to lean my chair back on two legs. Then my brain can think about balancing as well as whatever I'm doing sitting there, and I'm more relaxed about eating or writing or whatever.

Like most kids, I enjoy the big bounces some kids have at birthday parties. My Aunt Jean in Texas has a big trampoline in her yard, and I loved it even when I was two years old. I like to bounce on beds and sofas, too. Asperger's brains somehow feel better after bouncing, but scientists don't know why yet. Some people have become excellent gymnasts after starting out on a balanced chair, a sofa or a trampoline.

Other things I do when I want to comfort myself aren't as ordinary as changing the subject or balancing and bouncing. In fact, I have been told that these things are weird. I like to

whirl around or flap my hands.

Some kids and grown-ups who don't know about Asperger's have tried to make me stop. My parents help me understand what other people might think is odd. I am trying to make these movements smaller and to learn more usual ways to make my brain feel good.
Ever since I was little, I've had another way to comfort myself. Like most other people,

I love to be hugged, and I love to hug and lean against people for comfort.

Being squeezed like this feels really good to me, and I usually make other people feel good when I hug them. I like to say, "Give me a big Goran hug!" But sometimes I have confused people by hugging or kissing without asking. I am trying to learn to ask or to extend my arms in a big "let's hug" gesture, so that people can say if they don't want a hug right then.

This may seem odd to you because I also need to have my space. Sometimes I just want to be left alone. Touching me, restraining me, or even hugging me might make me feel as bad as teasing does. What I really need is to feel in control.

Here are other ways I get squeezes. When it's raining, I get under my mom's raincoat. At school, when it's too loud for me, or if I'm asked to do something uncomfortable, I make myself feel better by pulling my head and my arms or my legs into my shirt, or I crouch under my desk. I get under the table in restaurants, too, or I burrow behind my dad's back in a restaurant booth. At the movies, sometimes I hide my head during parts I think are scary. All this feels warm and cozy like a badger in its hole.

Dr. Temple Grandin, who has Asperger Syndrome, is an expert on large farm animals. When she was little, she found some squeezes very comforting for her. Later, she thought that cattle and horses might feel the same way. Now she goes all over the world designing livestock chutes that comfort animals rather than scare them. By calming herself, she learned how to calm the animals!

When I was little, I had a little nook in the corner of my room so that I could look at books quietly. I like to find tight, quiet places.

MY FIVE SENSES

People with Asperger's need to learn to make themselves more comfortable. We have very, very keen senses because of our **neurosystem** – the way our brains are built. Some doctors have compared people with this kind of disorder to dolphins because we have such keen senses.

Sight. Grown-ups sometimes think I'm not showing respect because I don't always want to look right in their eyes – "maintain eye contact", they call it. I want them to understand that my eyes work differently from most other people's. In fact, I hear people better when I don't look at them; looking and listening is sometimes just too much for me. Remember that I think better when I balance my chair on two legs while I do other things. I often work a puzzle or look at a book while watching a video, and I do both just fine. (But my mom won't let me watch and do homework at the same time!)

I do have 20/20 (normal) vision, but I don't see some things the same way my friends seem to. Catching a ball, for instance, isn't my best talent. And something about me makes me print all capital letters with no spaces between the words. This makes my work hard to read, and my parents and teachers are thinking of special ways to help me produce writing that you and my teachers can read more easily. (Asperger's kids often have accommodations in school because of their special talents and needs.) But I do have a great sense of color, line, and shape when I do my art. And I have great hand-eye coordination in small movements – you should see me play computer games or Game Boy or my Nintendo 64!

Hearing. *Loud hurts.* Like my sight, my hearing isn't typical. Sounds that other people think are ordinary are so loud that they drive me nuts! This happens to me a lot. One time in first grade, everybody was dropping dice onto hard surfaces during math time. I had to withdraw to the very corner of the room even to think straight.

At my old school, I hated the noisy cafeteria and always took my lunch from home so that I could eat on the yard. I don't much like singing in groups, and I can't stand the shrieks of the blender and the cappuccino maker. When I was little, I couldn't be in the bathroom when the toilet was being flushed. In Colorado, I visited a gold mine, where I used a pick to get some gold. But when they started using a jackhammer, I had the sense to excuse myself and go outside. At Cirque du Soleil, the band was too loud, so I curled up and fell asleep.

Loud is fun. Other times, I'm glad to be in loud places. My favorite restaurants are Dive! in Century City and I Cugini on Ocean Avenue. Movie sound technicians would call both of these places very "acoustically live" – that means really loud! (But if the noise at Dive! or I Cugini gets too much for me, I curl up and nap.)

What about my other senses? **Smell**. I'm usually not bothered by strong smells any more than ordinary people are.

Taste. And as for the sense of taste, all people lose taste buds as they grow older and have their strongest taste buds when they are young, so I don't like spicy foods any more than lots of kids I know. Two of my favorite foods are pasta with butter and pears, both mild-tasting foods.

Even though I don't have trouble with taste, I do need to eat on a fairly regular schedule. I've been known to get cranky, screaming, and aggressive when I'm hungry or thirsty. I'm trying to recognize my hunger and thirst before they get crucial – really important – and to ask politely if it's okay to eat and drink now.

Speech. I often talk more *slowly* than lots of other people do, and I pronounce each word carefully.

Sometimes I speak more *loudly* than most other people would in the same situation. Often my nose makes ticking noises that I can't help making. I have a big vocabulary because I read a lot and watch a lot, and maybe because I don't have any brothers or sisters, so I spend a lot of time with grown-ups. Big vocabularies, too, are typical of Asperger's people.

I imitate what I read and watch. But I also imitate real-live people. Often, when I make a mistake, I laugh and say "I'm stupid!" just like my ex-classmate Aaron, and when I feel impatient, I say "You've made your point," just like my dad.

Confused senses. Sometimes I have trouble making my senses work together. At I Cugini once, somebody at another table used the word "milk," and I said, "She called me 'Milk'!" Or when teachers speak or look at me, I may not know that they mean me. Just last Sunday on a whale watch, the ocean waves and bright sun and boat motor were too hard for me to process. Can you guess how I responded? Look at the next page.

You guessed it! I went to sleep. A few of the other Asperger's kids on board did, too. (I had seen a few whales before nodding out, though.)

Though I do talk somewhat slowly, I talk a lot. I love to tell of my most recent mania, and since I read well I know a lot about whatever is obsessing me at the moment. Some people call us Asperger's kids "little professors" because we seem to go on and on about our interests. These days, I am interested in these things: **Nintendo 64**, the comic hero Tintin, and manatees.

- ○ If ever there comes a time when you don't want to hear about my favorite subjects, I will try to understand that you don't, but I want you to ask me nicely to stop and not make me feel embarrassed or teased.

★ ★ ★ ★ ★ ★

As we become friends, you may notice me curling up, hiding in my shirt, balancing on my chair, losing my temper, spinning, making ticking noises, or talking on and on about my own interests. Now you know why I do those things!

Some things I can change about myself, and I am trying to change. Some things I cannot change about myself, and I am happy with them.

WHAT I DO WELL ALREADY, AND WHAT I NEED HELP DOING

My dad says I'll be a movie director or a theatrical director some day. **I do like to run the show!** My parents are usually happy to play parts in my dramas, and for the most part, my parents follow my directions pretty well.

But kids don't always. Last fall, I directed kids in a play at the UCLA play group I belong to, and those actors weren't nearly as cooperative! I have trouble concentrating on someone else's directions, but I can do it if I try. Here I am in a play. It was put on by my "Be-an-Actor" group last spring. I played a baby harp seal.

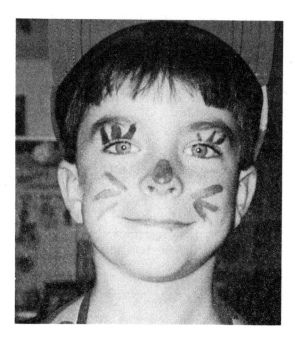

Max as a harp seal

If I like a thing, I like to think it through and plan it well. I like to play the games chess and checkers and "Guess Who?" and "Stratego." Often, I can beat my parents. But last Saturday at the Pokémon tournament, I lost on the first round, and I left the table angrily. Some people tell me I'm not a good winner. But I'm trying to be polite when I win – and cheerful whenever I don't.

I have strong feelings about fairness and justice, but my feelings may not seem fair to you. I'm very sensitive to what people say about **me**, but I say exactly what I think about **other people**.

The sixth sense – the social sense. Because I watch movies, have play dates, and hang out with my mom and dad, who teach me facial expressions, I can usually tell when someone likes me and wants to be friends, or is teasing me, which I definitely do not like.

But on the other hand, **sometimes I don't understand what people mean** by the expression on their faces or the tone of their voices. Maybe someone is angry with me or doesn't want to play with me, but I can't tell. Maybe someone is complimenting me or asking me to join a group, but I'm not sure.

What I need is for people to include me even when I seem out of it.

Many older people seem to think that I should naturally know what people mean. But people with Asperger's don't always know right away. That's because most people learn naturally what Asperger's people have to be taught.

What I need is for people to help me learn even more than I do already about facial expressions and tone of voice.

Jokes and fun. A few people with Asperger's Syndrome don't understand word play very well, but I usually do. If someone says it's "raining cats and dogs", I know that's just an expression. Or if someone tells a good "knock-knock" joke, I can laugh at the punch line. **My favorite knock-knock is hard to write down on paper, so ask me what it is, and I'll tell you.**

Then maybe you can tell me a joke.

_____

_____

_____

_____

In fact, I like word play. I just made up two songs for the cafeteria: "We All Live in a Yellow Submarine **Sandwich**" and "It Had to Be **Stew**." Here is another cafeteria joke I just made up: When do steaks say hello? When they meet! Meat and meet. Get it?

I really like this joke. I heard it on Rosie O'Donnell's TV show the only time I watched it. I really like to tell this joke out loud with lots of expression.

A duck comes into a bar and says, "Ya got any grapes?" The bartender says, "No, this is a bar. We don't sell grapes."

The duck goes outside and comes back. He says, "Ya got any grapes?" The bartender says, "No, this is a bar. We don't sell grapes. If you ask me that again, I'll staple your feet to the floor."

The duck goes outside and comes back. He says, "Ya got any staples?" The bartender says, "No."

So the duck says, "Ya got any grapes?"

Even though I don't much like group singing, I do love music. People tell me I have an amazing memory for musical themes. But my hatred of singing in a group means that I really don't like it if someone picks up a tune I'm humming and hums along with me. But this has made me invent a favorite trick I play on people. I start humming a memorable but annoying song. This puts it into their heads, and then they can't get it out all day. My dad hates a Looney Tune tune called "Food Around the

Corner", and my mom doesn't like the "Winnie-the-Pooh" theme song. (Are you singing "Winnie-the-Pooh" to yourself right now?)

I like things to happen over and over again.

That's one reason I like science so much. Although there is always something new, science has laws that you can rely on.

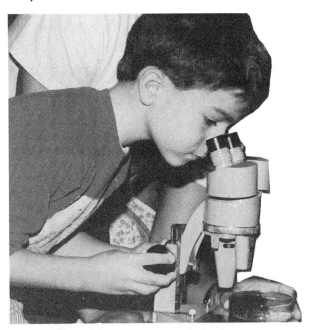

I like to know what's going to happen ahead of time.

That's one reason I like to watch the same movies over and over again. Lately I have been watching the **Star Wars** remastered trilogy a lot and an old black-and-white movie called **The Mark of Zorro**, which is about a Robin Hood-type hero in long-ago Los Angeles. I can memorize most of my favorite movies' words and music. I like knowing the beginning and the end of the story and what comes next. **Movies I can predict; live people can be harder**.

I love to play with my computer. Right now my favorite games are "Treasure Galaxy" and "Jewel Chase". I have several computer disks, such as "Pajama Sam: No Need to Hide When It's Dark Outside", "Myst", and "3-D Architect". At my old school, I would also play "Yukon Trail" and "SimCity 2000". I have "Mario 64", "Yoshi's Story", and "Diddy Kong Racing."

CONTROL OVER POWER; OR, WHY I LIKE KARATE

Max in his **gi**

I have started taking karate at the United School of Self-Defense in Pacific Palisades. Jim is a black belt, the highest honor you can get, and he is my **sensei** – my teacher. I am having so much fun that I sometimes forget that I'm also learning more self-respect and more coordination! Jim says that my concentration is way, way up now.

I can't show you the moves I am learning because if you don't know karate you might use the moves incorrectly and hurt yourself or another person. Here I am in my **gi**, or karate uniform.

On the back of my **gi** is a picture of a tiger, one of the five symbolic animals in karate. I chose the tiger because it represents strength and speed and because it is cool-looking.

Another karate animal I want to imitate is the dragon. It is the only karate animal that can work on land, on the sea, and in the air. **The dragon represents flexibility**, which is a really important quality I am working to have myself. I like to do art about dragons.

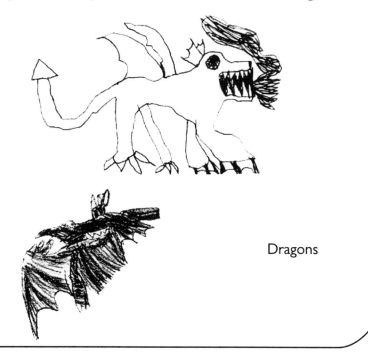

Dragons

Karate is teaching me yet another thing: One of the main symbols of karate is open-hand-over-fist. The fist symbolizes power; the open hand symbolizes control: **control over power**.

I am trying to have more self-control rather than throwing tantrums, dropping to the floor, striking out at other people, or shouting something I've heard in a movie. But remember that this control is hard for me because I have an Asperger's brain.

MY GOALS AND MY PLANS

I have a special educational plan with goals I'm trying to meet. One of these is to recognize when I'm beginning to get upset or angry. Sometimes I get upset at home because things aren't going my way or because I'm not getting all the attention I want or because my parents or my pets aren't giving me my space.

When I start feeling bad, I think I might upset people around me or embarrass myself.

So my plan is either to drop to the floor quietly, or to leave the room quietly and find my quiet "safe place" until I've cooled down.

I'm lucky because I get to have this special way to cool down. My family is working on that goal at home, too.

I'm glad that Franklin School has a program called "How Does Your Engine Run?" that helps me learn more about my six senses, making myself comfortable, and plans to make my classrooms better for learning for everybody.

I think that most people, not just me, need to recognize when they're getting steamed up. I think that most people need a "safe place" to be private and calm and comfortable. When I'm over the mad feeling, once in a while I want to talk about what made me mad, but usually I just want to get over it and forget it.

Some kids with Asperger's learn to read very young. A kid I know named Dominique could read before he could talk. When I was in kindergarten, I became an independent reader. I scored 24, whatever that means, but my friend Julia tells me it is the highest you can get in kindergarten, and she was the only other kid who did. Nobody pushed me to read, but ever since I was a tiny baby, my parents always read to me every day. They made funny voices and special rhythms and other stuff to make the story extra good. Now we read together, or I read to them instead.

I am glad I can read. At home, I have hundreds of books and I subscribe to several magazines, and I can find comfort by reading. Here I am in my room at home:

Often, when things get hard for me in the classroom, quietly I slip over to the room library and use it as a second "safe place."

My goal is to be able to participate in class as often as I can.

But I will never want to stop reading.

One of the biggest things that I want to learn is how to recognize a true friend from a false one. Some kids with typical brains take advantage of kids with non-typical brains by asking them to do silly things to earn their friendship, or making fun of them behind their backs.

The thing I hate the very most is to be embarrassed, and I think most people don't like being embarrassed, too. True friends do not take advantage of other people.

I feel like I have had lots of friends in my life, and people have liked me because I have interesting things to say. Even though I like repetition, one of the reasons I am fun is that I am unpredictable and entertaining.

THANK YOU

Asperger Syndrome is one of the autism spectrum disorders. Some people believe that people with autism spectrum disorders don't want friends. But that is not true! I like kids to like me, and as far as I know, the nice ones do.

What I really want at Franklin School and for my entire life is to be happy and to have friends. I think that we are alike in that way, and I want to be your friend.

Thank you for reading my book.

Your friend,

★ ★ ★

Thumbs-up reviews

Grown-ups received "advance copies" of the book before the new classmates had seen it or met its author. A week before Max was to enter his new school, we all went for a meeting in the principal's office, along with Regional Center education advocate Barbara Marbach, who had been both strategist and hand-holder during our family's 18 months of hostilities with the district. We distributed the book to the group, an impressive assembly: district special education coordinator, principal, special ed teacher, general ed second-grade teacher, speech pathologist, school psychologist. As any author desires, and as we as collaborative authors had hoped, the book touched this audience; "What a labor of love!" they said, and "Now this is impressive." Through mediation – more than once, with different attorneys – Mom and Dad had established themselves with the district as hard-working, savvy and relentless. The book advertised us all as hard-working, obliging and caring. In dispute with the district, we could not have risked this new intimacy between author and audience.

The peer-reviews of Max's book reflected this new atmosphere. They were sweet though sparse: five of the students in a class of 19, two girls and three boys, wrote welcome letters to Max, as his book suggests. "I can be your friend. Look for me at recess," said one boy. Max responded, dictating letters to each student to Mom at the keyboard. "Dear Laura," he wrote to another student. "Thank you for wanting to be my friend. Thank you for drawing a picture of yourself. I like to read, too."

But the book didn't stand alone. Like a lot of published authors, Max had public relations help. The school psychologist and the district inclusion coordinator spoke with the children about Max, and learned that many of the kids had thought that Max "doesn't like us", he was so isolated and, at times, disagreeable. Though Max chose to be out of the room during these presentations, he made his wishes known about their content – what could be added to the book and what couldn't, what information from the book should be omitted.

The book wound up in a number of places. The $30 color photocopy version of the booklet was lent to a renouned linguist studying communication by children with autism. Black-and-white "teacher's editions" found their way to additional administrators and specialists. Linda Andron took a copy to show her graduate students. Later that same year, we used the book to brief a new sitter about Max's special requirements, and we made a gift of the book for the departing sitter and other family members and friends. People beyond Max's daily associates got copies of the book, too. As Dad and Mom planned a will and a probate-avoiding family trust, we asked a Midwest uncle to be Max's guardian; the uncle knows Max, of course, but our book provided a realistic, focused summary to help the uncle decide whether to accept our request. Finally, we sent copies to some of those who had inspired our book: Karen L. Simmons in Canada and the ALERT Program in Albuquerque.

As students, our primary audience, genuinely included Max as a peer, reactions to Max normalized. During second and third grades, Max became a school poster boy for inclusion. The classroom tenor evolved from wariness about him – "He doesn't like us" – to interaction with him – "Let me help, Max." This caretaking mode continues, as it should and probably will, for he isn't meeting his benchmarks for an IEP goal to submit his homework and store his stuff in the right places. But Max does know how to lead small-group discussions about literature, direct and star in class skits and plays, participate in games and relays in regular PE, and function effectively as a class officer ("Environmental Engineer" – responsible for encouraging students to recycle scrap from the floor and their desks). How happy his third-grade general ed teacher was when she heard a new friend, Alex, react to Max with routine, ordinary annoyance: "Cut it out, Max!"

"Hi. I'm Max" Redux

As Max entered fourth grade in Fall 1999, he wanted more re-sponsibility for introducing himself to his classmates. The teacher, who emphasizes social skills, mutual respect and the classroom "community" for all of her students, knew Max's AS autobiography by reputation and wanted to use it for a "community circle." This second edition required updates. Mom abridged the booklet for oral reading. Max revised, too, adding some new topical details and audience queries – favorite video games, favorite movies, favorite books – and left the photographs and artwork at home. During the circle reading, Alex, the third grade pal, affirmed one or another of the booklet's descriptions. And sometimes, Max himself added an *ex cathedra* remark. "I don't lose my temper anymore if I haven't eaten," he told the class.

Mom and Dad are far more canny now, rely more on our gut emotions about teachers, recognize the red-flag of "I believe in inclusion as much as anybody, but . . .". Max feels loyal to the new school. He respects and likes both the special ed staff and his classroom teachers. He attends weekly "snack club", a social skills group composed of several fourth-graders. Various accommoda-tions still must happen, and though Max still loves story-telling, he's learning keyboarding because he finds the small-motor task of writing down the stories tedious. He has friends among both special and typical kids, has many play-dates, and is invited to birthday parties and sleepovers – the usual benchmarks of suc-cessful friend-making in inclusive settings.

Complementing this considerable achievement is Max's continued self-awareness and ability at narrative and argument. He has grown in his ability to stand up for himself, to try to un-derstand others' motivations, and to articulate the principles of justice in an interaction. He can analyze the normative practice in a new community, but perhaps even more important, he is learning to speak across discourse communities, endeavoring to make connections between his own interests and those of other people, one of the most difficult operations for anybody, especially for AS people. Look at Max's communicative achievement through the eyes of Jim Sinclair, who in "Don't Mourn For Us" describes his own life-long rhetorical and social situation:

> It takes more work to communicate with someone whose native language isn't the same as yours... [But] we spend our entire lives doing it... Each of us who manages to reach out and make a connection with you... is operating in alien territory, making contact with alien beings. We spend our entire lives doing this. And then you tell us that we can't relate.

Although Mrs X, the benighted second-grade teacher, professed to love children, hers was not an active, inclusive love. Rather, it's special kids and their collaborators who have developed the power to communicate across boundaries not of their own making.

References

Forest , M. and Pearpoint, J. (1995) *Inclusion: The Bigger Picture.* Toronto: Inclusion Press.

Lunsford, A. and Ruszkiewicz, J. (1998) *Everything's an Argument.* New York: St. Martin's Press.

Simmons, K.L. (1996) *Little Rainman: Autism – Through the Eyes of a Child.* Arlington, TX: Future Horizons.

Sinclair, J. (1993) "Don't Mourn for Us." *Our Voices. Autism Network International 1,* 3. Also on Sinclair's web page: members.nbci.com/JimSinclair/

www.inclusion.com – information and insight about self-control and control of others; also links to other school and community topics for AS people and their families.

Appendix

Thank You for Trusting Me[1]

GLEN (Chapter 1)

Hi, my name is Glen. I am 11 and I am a sixth grader. I hope to become one of the great science minds of the world. I am an extremely smart person. Sometimes people don't understand this because I spend part of my day in a special education class for children with autism. Because of my autism I have trouble when there is a lot of noise. Therefore, I find it difficult to be in regular classes all the time.

Also, other children are somewhat different than me. Though my interests are normal, such as *Star Wars* and video games, they are more intense and sometimes I have a tendency to talk about them too much. Also it is hard for me to look at people sometimes and I fidget like I do not care what the other person is saying.

I do not like it when people discriminate against me. I am in an honors math class, but some people call me retarded. How could I be in an honors math class and be retarded? When I went into an honors science class the kids were quite mean and discriminated against me. However, when I came back into the class to show them my science project on ph indicators they were very

---

1 The monologues that follow are part of a video series, focusing on inclusion, produced by UCLA Family Support Community Program and distributed by Special Needs Project (see Resource List).

impressed and rated it very highly and then they didn't discriminate against me anymore.

I like myself and consider my difference something positive. However, I do not mind if people tell me how they feel as long as they tell me in an appropriate fashion. I don't like to be told I'm rude, but I'd rather have someone tell me how it makes them feel. You can say "Glen, when you don't look at me I don't feel like you are listening to me."

My brother and I are very funny people. Some people think that kids with autism do not have a sense of humor. But we do. "Those dang nuts them." We make up our plays like The Psychiatrist and The Seaside Journey and Discoll and Bebert. I also like to draw my own cartoons. I particularly like the Far Side and Dilbert. My comic strip is called Glen's strip. And that is all I have to say for this monologue.

EVAN (Chapter 1)

(In addition to his autism, Evan has been challenged with a brain tumor that required two surgeries and has left him with additional challenges. Evan is now 16, totally independent of his wheel chair, and about to go on a class trip to Italy.)

My name is Evan I am 14 years old and I am in the seventh grade. I am interested in world records, UFO's strange happenings, and things a lot of kids are interested in. I like to listen to popular music and I like to dress in clothes that are in.

When I was eight, I started to have problems. My right hand shook when I tried to use it so I had to start using my left hand. Then I found out that I had a brain tumor. I had to have surgery twice. Both times, after surgery, I couldn't walk very well for a while. I had to wear a helmet and use a walker. I still use a wheelchair if I have to go long distances, but most of the time I am like a typical kid except that I have some learning disabilities. In some ways I am really smart. I used to be really interested in geography and still know a lot about it.

I also know a lot about different cultures. I like Native American tribes and China, particularly. But I also have some things that are hard for me. My hand still shakes so my writing is wiggly and I still have to use a calculator to do math. I also like to think about questions for a long time before I answer them and I am very shy with people I don't know very well, so sometimes people think I am not intelligent. I don't talk a lot, but I like to watch people and listen to what they are saying. It is what anthropologists do. And sometimes I think maybe I will be an anthropologist when I grow up.

My disabilities aren't very obvious, but I hate when people call me weak. I know I am weak and I don't want to be. I want to be strong, I want to be normal. But mostly like everyone else I want to be happy and have a good life

JOSH (Chapter 2)

Hi my name is Josh. I am 12 years old and I have Asperger Syndrome. I was asked to tell you how to get along in a regular class.

- Sit and listen;
- Do what you are supposed to do in class;
- When you have free time do what you want to do. I draw;
- Make sure you can see in class and make sure you are comfortable;
- The thing that you need to do is not show your symptoms;
- Don't make all those rapid movements and don't act hyper;
- Make smaller movements;
- Breathe deeply;

- And move your toes, but not very big movements so people can notice.

If you can't do something you need to tell the teacher. I never learned to write using cursive style. So my parents helped by letting the teacher know that she needed to make an accommodation. She lets me print. I believe that parents should help by telling the teacher what changes they need to make and why but nothing else.

When I take math tests, I sometimes get nervous. I think that it is a race and I tense up. So I ask the teacher if I can take it home to finish, so that I will be more relaxed and comfortable.

If you are with a person for a long time, you talk with them and after a time you become good friends. I ask them questions about what they like. It helps if you like what they like. I ask them their opinions about things and I listen hard. Don't tell people you only like one type of something.

If someone is doing something wrong in class, just ignore them.

Finally, remember that the biggest challenge in life is to make a friend out of an enemy, I don't have a clue how to do that yet.

CHRIS

Hi, my name is Chris. I am 14 years old and in the seventh grade. I love to tell jokes. I like *Garfield, Calvin and Hobbes* and the *Peanuts Gang* comics. I really enjoy playing on the computer. I like to go to movies and really love amusement parks.

I am a little different from other kids. I have something called autism. Autism means that your brain is wired differently. It doesn't mean that you're disabled, it just means you're different. My autism helps me out in a lot of ways. When I go to Disneyland and other theme parks, I get a pass so I don't have to wait in line. My autism also helps memorize things and helps my brain keep information together in school. My autism doesn't have any bad effects on me. I like myself the way I am. I don't like it when kids tease me or try to talk me into doing things by saying they will be my friend. When I first started middle school, the kids tried to get me to dance. After a while I learned that they weren't really my friends and were just trying to embarrass me.

I have some nervous habits that sometimes bother people,. Like rubbing my face because I think I have crumbs on it, picking my nose, and forgetting that I put my hands in my pants. I don't really find it helpful for people to correct me. But if I do something that bothers people I don't mind if they tell me. You say "Chris, I really don't like when you do that." Or "Chris, it bothers me when you do that."

I think it is important for people to understand difference. When I told the other kids in my class about my differences they stopped teasing me and they helped other kids in the school to understand. The only thing you need to do to help kids with autism is to treat them with respect and understand that they have certain things that they can do really well.

ALEXIS

(Alexis' primary diagnosis was cri du chat, technically known as 5P-. Over the years ADHD, OCD, and Tourette's syndrome have been added. Alexis was recently evaluated by Dr Anthony Attwood, who felt she also had AS. He indicates that the presence of these four disorders together is a pattern that he has seen in many children.)

My name is Alexis I am twelve and a half years old and in the sixth grade. I love to read, play with my dog, play with my two chickens and watch TV. I read at least one book a day. My favorite shows are *Kablam* and the *Real Adventures of Johnny Quest*. I am really interested in the movies. I know a lot about movies because my dad is a producer. I like to count advertisements. I can tell when a movie is getting less popular, by the size of the advertisement in the paper. I read the calendar section of the *LA Times* every day. When I am out of town my family do not throw out the

Calendar section or recycle it, they wait until I get home so I can read it.

I have a really good memory. I usually know the answers to most of the questions the teachers ask in class. My memory also helps me to remember things about movies and other things I am interested in. I love candy and I love practical jokes.

I am a little different from other kids. I have a disability. It's called 5 P-. It is something in my genes. It makes me grow slower than other kids so I am kind of small. It also makes my voice high and kind of squeaky. Sometimes I don't understand social situations too well and people think that I am retarded. Kids ignore me and sometimes they tease me. It makes me feel horrible, lonely and mad. Sometimes I do things that are kind of embarrassing. Like I wanted to win the prize for recycling so I went into the garbage cans during lunch to collect soda cans. I don't mind if people point out that these behaviors bother them, but I would like them to tell me quietly.

Sometimes I just like to be by myself and read or draw in my sketch book, but I would like if someone came up and offered to sit by me. Besides, I am not always into the things that other kids are talking about, but I do listen.

In conclusion, I am just like other kids but I need to learn things that most kids learn without even knowing. To all the kids like me who have a disability and are going to be in a class with normal kids, my advice is that you tell the cool kids that you are not retarded, just a little different. If you do this, like I did, you will have a better life. To all those kids who are normal, if you are honest and tell about your difficulties you will have a better life too.

DAVID

(David is now 11 and attending a private school that uses laptops for all subjects. In addition to ADHD and Tourette's, David was later diagnosed with OCD. He was recently seen by Dr Attwood who felt that AS was also present and explained the social piece of David's difficulties.)

My name is David. I am 9 years old. I have Attention Deficit Hyperactivity Disorder and Tourette's Syndrome. I also have a non-verbal learning disorder. What this means is that I have trouble in school, paying attention, sitting in my seat, and doing long written assignments. When things get really tough, I get tics like eye twitches, grunting or shrugging my shoulders. Right now I go to a gifted magnet in public school. I am at the end of third grade this year. I have an aide who helps me in the classroom. He helps me stay on track a lot better.

Sometimes I still have a hard time and I have a tantrum or I start crying. When this happens there are people at school who can help me. When I am having a hard time, the worst thing the kids can do is tease me. This makes me feel sad. Instead I would just like them to be my friends and be nice to me.

Resource List

Asperger Syndrome Coalition of the United States (ASC-US)
P.O. Box 49267
Jacksonville Beach, FL 32240-9267
Tel: (904)-745-6741
www.asperger.org

ASC-US is a national non-profit organization committed to providing the most up-to-date and comprehensive information on social and communication disorders, with particular focus on Asperger Syndrome and Non-verbal Learning Disorder.

Autism Society of America,
7910 Woodmont Ave, Suite 300
Bethesda, MD 20814-3015
Tel: (800)-3AUTISM x 150
 (301)-657-0881
Fax: (301)-657-0869
www.autism-society.org

The mission of the Autism Society of America is to promote lifelong access and opportunities for persons within the autism spectrum and their families, to be fully included, participating members of their communities through advocacy, public awareness, education, and research related to autism.

Family & Advocates Partnership for Education (FAPE)
PACER Center 4826
Chicago Ave. S.
Minneapolis, MN 55417-1098
Tel: (888)-248-0822
fape@pacer.org
www.fape.org

The Family & Advocates Partnership for Education (FAPE) website is a new project which aims to inform and educate families and advocates about the Individuals with Disabilities Education Act of 1997 and promising practices.

More Advanced Individuals with Autism, Asperger's Syndrome and Pervasive Developmental Disorder (MAAP)

Maap Services, Inc.
P.O. Box 524
Crown Point, IN 46308 USA
Tel: (219)-662-1311
Fax: (219)-662-0638
www.maapservices.org

Maap Services, Inc. is a nonprofit organization dedicated to providing information and advice to families of more advanced individuals with autism, Asperger Syndrome, and pervasive developmental disorder (PDD). Through its quarterly newsletter, The Maap, the organization provides the opportunity for parents and professionals to network with others in similar circumstances and to learn about more advanced individuals within the autism spectrum.

The National Information Center for Children and Youth with Disabilities (NICHCY)

P.O. Box 1492
Washington, DC 20013
Tel: (800)-695-0285
www.nichcy.org

NICHCY is the national information and referral center that provides information on disabilities and disability-related issues for families, educators, and other professionals. Their special focus is children and youth (birth to age 22).

Special Needs Project

324 State Street, Suite H
Santa Barbara, CA 93101
Tel: (800)-333-6867
Fax: (805)-962-5087
http://www.specialneeds.com

Special Needs Project is a place to get books about disabilities. Located in Santa Barbara, California, SNP serves families, professionals, agencies and schools worldwide with the largest, most authoritative collection of disability-related materials. It is the distributor of "Thank You for Trusting Me" (see Appendix).

Useful Websites

Online Asperger Syndrome Information and Support (OASIS)

www.aspergersyndrome.org

Oops Wrong Planet! Syndrome

www.isn.net/~jypsy

www.tonyattwood.com

Dr Attwood's website has papers related to diagnosis and education of those with Asperger's and High Functioning Autism as well as links to other sites with helpful information.

www.aspie.com

This is a wonderful website hosted by Liane Holliday Willey.

www.oceansofemotions.com

Oceans of Emotions has many products to assist in helping children with autism and Asperger Syndrome with emotional development. These include "taylor-made" games that focus on the specific issues of a child and their family. Therapist and classroom versions of the games are also available. Other products include *Flag Your Feelings,* and a series of products including stickers, posters, cards and a bingo game featuring cartoon faces of feelings. They are working closely with Dr Tony Attwood to develop new products, including a Feel-O-Meter and journals and other booklets for affective education.

Subject Index

Author Index